CAMBRIDGE

T0363839

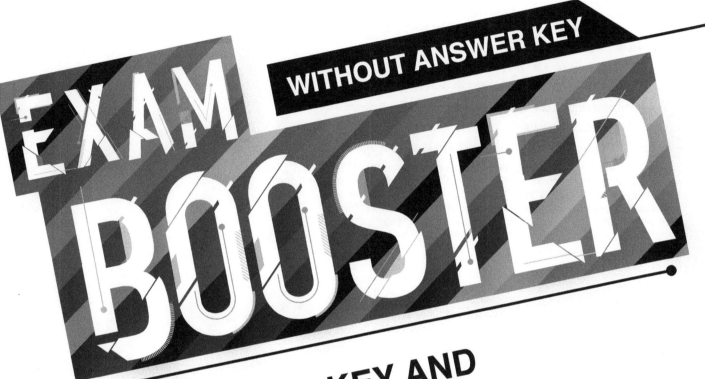

WITHOUT ANSWER KEY

EXAM BOOSTER

FOR A2 KEY AND A2 KEY FOR SCHOOLS

Second edition

WITH AUDIO

Comprehensive exam practice for students

Caroline Chapman, Susan White and Sarah Dymond

For the revised exams from 2020

Cambridge University Press
www.cambridge.org/elt

Cambridge Assessment English
www.cambridgeenglish.org

Information on this title: www.cambridge.org/9781108682268

First published 2020

20 19 18 17 16 15 14 13 12 11

Printed in Great Britain by CPI Group (UK) Ltd, Croydon CR0 4YY

A catalogue record for this publication is available from the British Library

ISBN 978-1-108-68226-8

Additional resources for this publication at www.cambridge.org/a2keybooster

CONTENTS

MAP OF THE BOOK

Reading and Writing 60 minutes	Worksheet 1	Worksheet 2	Worksheet 3
Reading and Writing Part 1 p6 3-option multiple choice 6 questions 6 marks	**Daily life** Present simple and adverbs of frequency Daily routine questions	**Places and buildings** Places vocabulary Asking for and giving information	**Services** Services vocabulary Understanding signs and notices
Reading and Writing Part 2 p12 3-option multiple matching 7 questions 7 marks	**The natural world** Landscape vocabulary Expressing agreement and disagreement	**Education and study** School subjects vocabulary Past simple and past events	**Travel and holidays** Travel vocabulary Directions
Reading and Writing Part 3 p18 3-option multiple choice 5 questions 5 marks	**Social interaction** Questions Responding to invitations	**Feelings, opinions and experiences** Present perfect + *just, yet, already, never, ever, for* and *since*	**Hobbies and leisure** Hobbies vocabulary Understanding information
Reading and Writing Part 4 p24 3-option multiple choice cloze 6 questions 6 marks	**Sports and games** *Go, play* and *do* Past simple and past continuous	**Entertainment and media** Music vocabulary Suggesting, accepting and refusing	**Transport** Comparatives and superlatives Making predictions
Reading and Writing Part 5 p30 Open cloze 6 questions 6 marks	**Daily life** Present simple and daily routine Email describing typical day	**Social interaction** Modals: possibility, ability and permission Present continuous and time expressions	**Travel and holidays** Using correct verb forms Holiday plans
Reading and Writing Part 6 p36 Guided writing 1 question 15 marks	**Health and exercise** Mixed tenses Writing an email	**Personal identification** Family vocabulary Giving personal information	**Entertainment and media** Entertainment vocabulary Using punctuation
Reading and Writing Part 7 p42 Picture story 1 question 15 marks	**Food and drink** Restaurant vocabulary Ordering events in a story	**Clothes** Things to wear Pronouns Useful expressions in a story	**The weather** Weather vocabulary Talking about the weather
Listening 30 minutes	**Worksheet 1**	**Worksheet 2**	**Worksheet 3**
Listening Part 1 p48 3-option multiple choice 5 questions 5 marks	**Services and places** Times, days and dates Places in town vocabulary	**Shopping and numbers** Numbers Shopping vocabulary	**Education and study** Present, future and past actions Daily routine

Listening Part 2 p54 Gap fill 5 questions 5 marks	**Making plans** Time vocabulary and prepositions of time *Going to* and *will*	**Health, medicine and exercise** Parts of the body vocabulary Modals of advice	**Dates and services** Dates, months and events Giving the time, day or date
Listening Part 3 p60 3-option multiple choice 5 questions 5 marks	**Leisure time** Giving information about days, dates, times and prices Free time vocabulary	**Social media and technology** Digital world vocabulary Present and past simple passive	**Travel and holidays** Documents and texts vocabulary Talking about future plans
Listening Part 4 p66 3-option multiple choice 5 questions 5 marks	**House and home** Home vocabulary Word order in questions	**Entertainment and the media** Opinion adjectives Jobs in entertainment/leisure Imperatives	**Education and study** Expressing rules Modals of obligation
Listening Part 5 p72 Matching 5 questions 5 marks	**Food and drink** *This, that, these* and *those* Countable and uncountable	**Hobbies and shopping** Likes and preferences Offers and requests	**Countries and sports** Languages and nationalities Suggestions and responding
Speaking **8–10 minutes**	**Worksheet 1**	**Worksheet 2**	**Worksheet 3**
Speaking Part 1 p78 Examiner asks questions 3–4 minutes	**Personal identification** Giving information about yourself Family vocabulary	**Daily life** Time expressions Word order and adverbs of frequency	**Places and buildings** Places in town vocabulary Talking about places you go to
Speaking Part 2 p84 Phase 1 Candidates discuss together Phase 2 Examiner asks questions 5–6 minutes	**Hobbies and leisure** Giving information about routines Seasons and months	**Sport** Action verbs Giving opinions	**Travel and holidays** Transport vocabulary Mixed tenses

Think about it p90

Exam topic lists p98

Go to https://www.cambridgeenglish.org/exams-and-tests/key-for-schools/ and https://www.cambridgeenglish.org/exams-and-tests/key/ for useful information about preparing for the A2 Key and A2 Key for Schools exams.

Daily life

✓ **Exam task**

For each question, choose the correct answer.

1

1

 **Rainbow Café**

Our popular breakfasts are served all day at excellent prices!

Healthy breakfasts also available.

A You can order this meal at any time.

B This café serves only healthy food.

C It's cheaper to eat here at less busy times.

2

Katie,
Are you free to go into town tomorrow? I need to get Tamara a birthday present. You always know what she likes.
Sam

7:16 p.m.

Sam is asking Katie

A to go into town with Tamara.

B to come to Tamara's birthday party.

C to help choose a gift for Tamara.

3

✉ **EMAIL**

Thank you for booking an appointment at Create Hairdressers.

Please arrive 10 minutes before your appointment time to discuss what you'd like us to do.

A Customers may only have to wait 10 minutes to get an appointment.

B Customers are asked to get to the hairdressers 10 minutes early.

C Customers who arrive more than 10 minutes late could lose their appointment.

4

Ted,

I've gone to pick up Lucy from her dance class and will make us all a snack when we get back at 8 p.m.

Mum

A Ted's mum has already eaten this evening.

B Ted's mum plans to prepare a light meal later.

C Ted's mum is cooking dinner before Lucy's dance class.

5

 Please check your receipt before leaving the shop and tell the assistant if there is a problem.

A Let the assistant know if you think there's a mistake on your receipt.

B Keep your receipt because you might need to change something you bought.

C Tell the assistant if you've lost the receipt for something you bought.

6

 Ken's Cakeshop

We're closed early today for cleaning.

Open again normal times
(9 a.m.-6 p.m.) tomorrow (Tuesday).

A The shop plans to change its usual opening times.

B The shop closes earlier on Mondays than Tuesdays.

C The shop will be open as usual from Tuesday.

2a Put the adverbs in the box in the correct order, from the most frequent (5) to the least frequent (1).

sometimes .... never .... often ....
always .... usually ....

2b Rewrite the sentences with the words or expressions in brackets in the correct place.

1. My brother plays tennis. (once a week)

....

2. Do you have breakfast? (always)

....

3. I drive to work. (every day)

....

4. I visit my sister at the weekend. (often)

....

5. I go to bed before midnight. (never)

....

6. My family eat dinner at 6 p.m. (usually)

....

3 Write the questions. Then write your answer below using an adverb of frequency.

1. time | usually | get up? ....

....

2. get up | different | time | at the weekend? ....

....

3. what | eat | for breakfast? ....

....

4. where | have | lunch? ....

....

 Exam facts

- In this part, you read six short texts. These are usually signs, notices, emails, text messages, notes or labels.
- For each question, you have to choose the sentence (A, B or C) that means the same as the text.

Places and buildings

1 Read the descriptions. Choose the correct answer, a, b or c.

1. You go here if you want to catch a plane.
   a station   **b** airport   **c** motorway

2. People go here to watch sports such as football.
   a roundabout   **b** theatre   **c** stadium

3. You can park your car in one of these.
   a garage   **b** lift   **c** underground

4. Businessmen and businesswomen work at desks in this place.
   a elevator   **b** pharmacy   **c** office

5. Parents take their children here so they can have fun.
   a playground   **b** market   **c** car park

6. Doctors and nurses work in this place.
   a guesthouse   **b** hospital   **c** factory

7. You can study lots of different subjects in this place.
   a college   **b** supermarket   **c** hotel

8. People work in this place and make things such as cars.
   a museum   **b** cafeteria   **c** factory

2 Complete the conversation with your own words.
Put ONE word in each space.

Receptionist: Good morning. Can I **(1)** .... you?

Nikki: Yes please. I **(2)** .... love to go to a museum. Is there one **(3)** .... this hotel?

Receptionist: Yes. You can walk to it from here. Just go out of the hotel, **(4)** .... left, walk for about ten minutes, and you will see it on your right.

Nikki: Thank you. **(5)** .... it a big museum?

Receptionist: Yes, it's the national museum. It's very large, and there's a lot to see there.

Nikki: That's great. I want to buy some postcards.
(6) .... the museum have a shop?

Receptionist: Yes, it has a very nice shop. It **(7)** .... books and gifts – and postcards, of course.

Nikki: Thank you very much for your help.

Receptionist: You're **(8)** .... ! Just ask me if you need anything else while you're staying here.

> ☑ **Exam tips**
>
> - Read each short text and think about where you might see it. Who has written it? Who is it for? What is it about?
> - Look for words or phrases in the sentences and the texts that have the same meaning.

3

For each question, choose the correct answer.

1

Leave shoes,
bags and towels in
changing rooms

There's no space
beside the pool

A The changing rooms are now in a different place.

B Swimmers can't take their stuff into the pool area.

C Don't forget your shoes, bags and towels before you go.

2

GUESTS

Please give room keys to
receptionist before leaving
hotel if you are checking out
or returning later.

A Guests should only return room keys on the last day of their visit.

B If there's no-one at reception, guests should keep their room keys with them.

C The hotel looks after the room keys when guests go out for the day.

3

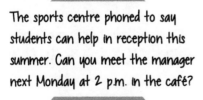

The sports centre phoned to say
students can help in reception this
summer. Can you meet the manager
next Monday at 2 p.m. in the café?

A The sports centre manager is looking for students to do reception work.

B There are summer jobs in the sports centre café starting from next week.

C The sports centre has holiday jobs for students to work as sports coaches.

4

Please use stairs
as lift not working

For customers with
children, nearest lift
20 metres

A There are no lifts working at the moment.

B This lift is only for people with children.

C Customers should take the stairs or another lift.

5

Visitor Notice

Please do not make or
take phone calls in the
hospital building

A Visitors' phones won't work inside the hospital building.

B Visitors should speak to hospital staff if they need to use a phone.

C Visitors mustn't use their phones anywhere inside the hospital.

6

Door on this floor for
staff only

Exit for museum visitors
on first floor

What does this notice say?

A The way out of the museum is on this floor.

B Visitors should use a different door to leave the museum.

C Ask a member of staff to show you where to leave the museum.

Services

1 Complete the sentences below with the words from the box.

bank	café	chemist	dentist	hotel
library	post office	tourist information		

1. I'm going to the .... to buy a stamp.
2. Is the .... open today? I need to get some cash.
3. My tooth hurts. I think I should make an appointment with my ....
4. I'm going to the .... to borrow a book about insects.
5. I've got my flight, but I still need to book a room in a .... for my holiday.
6. Is there a .... near here? I need to buy some medicine.
7. I booked a tour of the city at the .... centre.
8. Let's go to that new .... They make great hot chocolate.

2 Read the signs. Put the number in the correct part of the table.

Bank	Tourist information centre	Library
....	....	....

1. Please try to return books to the correct shelf. Thank you.

2. Need to find a room in a hotel? We can book one for you.

3. Information about train and bus times at this desk only.

4. Need to borrow money today? Speak to a member of staff.

5. DVDs £1.50 for one week.

6. Computer course for beginners. Starts Monday.

7. Lost your credit card? Call this number immediately. ☎ 970097 86809

8. Please pay for maps in cash.

3 For each question, choose the correct answer.

1

MOTORWAY CAFÉ

Please pay for hot drinks at cash desk, collect receipt and give it to serving staff, who will prepare your drink immediately.

A If you're only buying hot drinks, please pay in cash.

B The waiters will tell you how much to pay for your hot drinks.

C Collect your hot drinks after you have paid for them.

2

DENTIST

Ask the receptionist for our price list.
Appointments sometimes available on the day.

What does this notice say?

A There are still some appointments available for today.

B The dentist may see you if you haven't booked an appointment.

C When you book an appointment, we can't tell you how much it will cost.

3

TOURIST OFFICE

Free guidebooks and maps – ask inside.
Tours can also be booked here.

A Buy a guidebook from the tourist office.

B Collect a map from the tourist office.

C Tours leave from the tourist office.

4

✉ **EMAIL**

To: All students

Please return all books before the summer holiday. Speak to me if you think you have lost any books.
Mrs Deeks, School Library

A See Mrs Deeks if you can't find the books you borrowed.

B Tell Mrs Deeks if you plan to keep your library books until next term.

C Speak to Mrs Deeks if you don't know what to read during the holiday.

5

● ● ● ‹ › ⟳ ⌂

City Theatre
We cannot change your seats after you have booked tickets.

What can't theatre customers do?

A choose where they sit before they book

B get their money back on tickets

C ask for different seats after they've paid

6

James,
The new shopping centre's really big. You could spend the whole day there and not see all the shops. Let's meet there next Saturday.
Dan

7:16 p.m.

A Dan doesn't think they'll visit every shop in the shopping centre on Saturday.

B Dan doesn't think James will like the size of the shopping centre.

C Dan doesn't know how to get to the shopping centre.

 **Get it right!**

Look at the sentence below. Then try to correct the mistake.

The weather is very beautiful and I stay often on the beach.

The natural world

1   **Match each word in the box to the correct definition.**

desert	field	forest	island	lake	mountains	plants	river

1. a large area of water, often in a park ....
2. a very large area which has lots of trees in it ....
3. a piece of land with water all around it ....
4. trees and flowers are examples of these ....
5. a very dry area where it doesn't rain much ....
6. a long area of water that often ends in the sea ....
7. a farmer grows things or puts his animals here ....
8. these are very tall and often have snow at the top ....

☑ Exam facts

- In this part, you read three short texts.
- You have to answer seven questions.
- For each question, match the sentence to the correct text (A, B or C).

☑ Exam task

2   **Read the article about three people who are interested in nature.**
Answer the questions. For questions 1–7, choose A, B or C.

My love of nature

A   Sarah

When I was a child at school, I collected books about nature. My classmates and friends all spent their free time playing computer games, so to them I suppose I was a bit strange. I loved learning about animals from other countries, but as I got older I found out that my own country has interesting nature too, and that's what I like studying now. I do lots of drawings of nature, and I put them on my blog.

B   Pilar

I love birds and animals because of all the visits to forests and lakes we made when I was at school. It's a shame that things have changed so much now. In my opinion, children these days don't learn enough about nature, so lots of them are afraid of insects, for example. I have a great job because of my love of nature. I'm a nature photographer. It's brilliant, except for the early mornings!

C   Lia

A few years ago I read a blog with beautiful photos of animals, birds and plants, which made me start really looking at what lives around us. It was just a hobby at first, but now it's my job as I visit schools and give talks about nature. I love it. The only problem is if I am asked to draw a picture. I enjoy it, but I'm terrible at drawing! I'm going to take some lessons to try to get better.

1   Who became interested in nature from seeing someone else's blog?
    A Sarah   **B** Pilar   **C** Lia
2   Who says there is something about her job that she doesn't like?
    A Sarah   **B** Pilar   **C** Lia
3   Whose friends thought that her hobby was unusual?
    A Sarah   **B** Pilar   **C** Lia
4   Who became interested in nature because of school trips?
    A Sarah   **B** Pilar   **C** Lia
5   Who says that the type of nature she is interested in has changed?
    A Sarah   **B** Pilar   **C** Lia
6   Who wants to improve her pictures of nature?
    A Sarah   **B** Pilar   **C** Lia
7   Who thinks that young people should learn more about nature at school?
    A Sarah   **B** Pilar   **C** Lia

---

3   **Complete the conversation with phrases from the boxes.**

Adam: Do you live in a town, Ben?

Ben: No, in the countryside. And I love it.

Adam: **(1)** .... I lived in the countryside when I was a child, but I prefer towns.

Ben: Oh! Why is that?

Adam: Well, in the countryside you're so far away from schools, shops and friends' houses.

Ben: **(2)** .... You get more exercise because you have to walk more!

Adam: **(3)** .... You spend a lot of time in your car, driving everywhere!

Ben: But the traffic is much worse in towns. Towns are too noisy and busy.

Adam: **(4)** .... The countryside is boring!

Ben: **(5)** .... You can go walking, cycling, fishing – there are lots of things to do!

Adam: Yes – I can do them during short visits to the countryside! But I prefer to live in a town.

Ben: **(6)** .... I'm sure the view from my window is better than yours.

Adam: You're probably right. It's true that the countryside is beautiful, but I enjoy being with lots of people.

Ben: And that's what I hate!

Adam: Everyone is different, I suppose.

Ben: We certainly are!

Ben	**Adam**
a No, it isn't.	**d** No, you don't.
b Yes, but that's a good thing.	**e** Really? I don't understand that.
c Well, I don't.	**f** That's what I like!

Education and study

1 Complete the text below with the school subjects. Use the letters in brackets to help you.

There are lots of different subjects you can study at university. If you are good at **(1)** .... (gauselnag), you may decide to study French, Arabic or Chinese. If you like learning about how things work, then you probably find science subjects such as **(2)** .... (gibyolo), **(3)** .... (myshecrit) or **(4)** .... (shycips) interesting. People who are interested in things which happened a long time ago should study **(5)** .... (osriyth),

but if you prefer learning about rivers, mountains and the different countries of the world, then you should choose **(6)** .... (regopaygh). People who are good with numbers often decide to study **(7)** .... (shacamittem), and those who want to become doctors take a course in **(8)** .... (necmidei).

☑ Exam task

2 For each question, choose the correct answer.

My three favourite school subjects, by Annabelle Plume

A   Biology

I love biology because we discuss all kinds of important things. The time passes quickly in class and usually we don't finish our work before the end of the lesson. Then we have to take it home to do. That's OK because we download free videos and write notes about what we learn. Sometimes in class we use special equipment to do tests. I really enjoy this activity because we're allowed to choose who we work with, and my two best friends and I can be together.

B   Geography

I've always loved geography because I'm really interested in different places in the world. We sometimes go into the playground to draw the countryside around the school, but it's a pity we can't do trips to places like the beach or the mountains. The teacher gave everyone in the group a textbook to take home, but we had to get our own colouring pens and pay for a software program for drawing maps.

C   History

I didn't use to enjoy history that much, but now I love watching programmes about the subject in my free time. So far this year, our group has been to two museums, and I think we'll visit a few other places before the end of the year. At the moment, we're studying the history of medicine and learning about some very strange medicines and equipment. The teacher gives us information and we have to write lots of notes in our exercise books. If we want, we can draw a few pictures for homework.

1 Which subject offers students several trips?

   A biology   **B** geography   **C** history

2 Which subject includes working in small groups?

   A biology   **B** geography   **C** history

3 Which subject needs extra equipment that students have to buy?

   A biology   **B** geography   **C** history

4 Which subject has a lot of homework?

   A biology   **B** geography   **C** history

5 Which subject has some lessons outdoors?

   A biology   **B** geography   **C** history

6 Which subject teaches students about something unusual?

   A biology   **B** geography   **C** history

7 Which subject includes watching videos?

   A biology   **B** geography   **C** history

3   **Choose the correct form of the verb to complete each sentence.**

1. I *broken / break / broke* my pen yesterday.
2. When I was little I didn't *known / know / knew* how to write.
3. I *ridden / rode / ride* my new bike to college yesterday.
4. I was so tired when I got home from school that I *lain / lie / lay* down and fell asleep.
5. I *took / taken / take* my exams last week.
6. We *given / give / gave* our teacher a present at the end of the year.
7. Did you *saw / see / seen* your friend at college?
8. I didn't *go / went / gone* to school until I was seven years old.

☑ **Exam tips**

- Quickly read the texts before you answer the questions.
- The questions are not in the same order as the information in the texts.
- Read the questions and the texts carefully.
- Don't think an answer is right just because you see the same word in the text and the question.

Travel and holidays

1 Complete the advice about plane travel. The first letter of each word is given to help you.

If you are going to travel to a different country, you need to have a **(1)** p .... When you are packing, try not to put too much in your **(2)** l .... Try to get to the **(3)** a .... a few hours before your flight, so that you won't **(4)** m .... it, and so that you get a good **(5)** s .... on the plane. Take something to read, as there may be a **(6)** d .... if the flight is late, or if the weather is bad. During the flight, be polite to other **(7)** p .... and remember to listen to the instructions which the **(8)** p .... and other airline staff give you.

☑ Exam task

2 For each question, choose the correct answer.

My last holiday

A Max

I went on holiday with my friends. The flight was fine, but it took two hours by bus to get to the hotel – I didn't enjoy that! The hotel was noisy and the staff weren't friendly, but it didn't matter because we spent all our time on the beach, a short walk away. We tried lots of new dishes in the restaurants in the town. It was hard to sleep with such high temperatures, but we had a fantastic time, and the best thing was, we spent almost nothing once we arrived!

B Felipe

The drive to our hotel from the airport was along lovely country roads. The hotel my wife and I stayed in was quite expensive. The people who worked there were wonderful, but I wasn't so sure about the hotel restaurant – the desserts were fine, but the main courses weren't very good. It was cloudy and rainy most days, but it didn't matter at all because we went to walk in the countryside, not to lie on a beach.

C Nikhil

My family and I drove across the USA last year. We stayed in lots of different hotels. I don't know how much we spent because my parents paid. There was a lot of driving, but my dad enjoyed that. The weather was fantastic, and I couldn't believe the differences in what people ate from place to place. It was good to be with the family, because there was always someone to talk to, or to do things with.

1   Who was surprised about the variety of food on holiday?

   A Max   **B** Felipe   **C** Nikhil

2   Who thought that part of their journey was too long?

   A Max   **B** Felipe   **C** Nikhil

3   Who liked travelling with a group of people?

   A Max   **B** Felipe   **C** Nikhil

4   Who was happy with the cost of their holiday?

   A Max   **B** Felipe   **C** Nikhil

5   Who thought the hotel staff were good?

   A Max   **B** Felipe   **C** Nikhil

6   Who says that the weather was a problem at times?

   A Max   **B** Felipe   **C** Nikhil

7   Who was unhappy with some of the food they ate?

   A Max   **B** Felipe   **C** Nikhil

---

3   ◀)) Track 1 **Listen to the conversations. Are the sentences TRUE or FALSE?**

1. The woman needs to drive north to get to the airport. ....

2. The man needs to go straight on at the roundabout. ....

3. The restaurant is a long way from the hotel. ....

4. The man knows a faster way to get to the beach. ....

5. The man and the woman need to go south. ....

6. The man and the woman need to turn left to get to the market. ....

7. The hotel is on the road where the man already is. ....

8. The woman needs to turn right immediately. ....

◎ *Get it right!*

Look at the sentence below. Then try to correct the mistake.

I've seen my brother yesterday.

Social interaction

1 Complete the questions with the correct question word(s).

1. .... is that, sitting near the door?
2. .... do you come here? Once a week?
3. .... bag is that, on the chair?
4. .... of these songs shall we listen to first?
5. .... have you lived here?
6. .... do you think we should do?
7. .... did you buy that hat? I'd like to get one.
8. .... will we see you again?

☑ Exam facts

- In this part, you read a longer text.
- There are five questions and you have to choose the right answer (A, B or C).
- The questions test understanding of main ideas or detailed information.

☑ Exam task

2 For each question, choose the correct answer.

| HOME | FEATURES | ABOUT ME | CONTACT ME | | SEARCH |

13-year-old Alessandra talks about her favourite chatroom, Teen-Age

I joined a chatroom called Teen-Age last month. A classmate read about it in a magazine and told me all about it. She said it's a really great way to make friends with people in other countries. And she was right!

Everyone on the chatroom is a teenager. We share information about home life, music and films. Friends that I chat to often ask me about school life in Britain. One friend in Spain sometimes asks me to write the words of English songs for her. My favourite thing is finding out how to prepare food people eat in different countries.

Some of my friends on Teen-Age live on the other side of the world, so when I chat to them at lunchtime, it's nearly midnight where they are. My parents like it that I have international friends, but they get upset if I'm chatting to people all evening. They always want me to finish my homework first.

Chatting to people online is different from chatting to people at school. Some people at school aren't very friendly and don't want to talk much, but everyone I've met on Teen-Age is really nice. It's easy to talk about problems with them and they usually give good advice.

Many of my schoolfriends have joined several chatrooms, but I won't ever do that. I like the online friends I have now, so I'll keep using Teen-Age. If I have friends in different chatrooms, it'll be too hard to chat to them all.

1 How did Alessandra find out about the chatroom?

   A from a magazine

   B from someone at school

   C from a friend in another country

2 What does Alessandra like doing best on the chatroom?

   A learning new dishes

   B talking about music and films

   C finding out about schools around the world

3 What does Alessandra say about her parents?

   A They worry that she is chatting online while she is at school.

   B They think schoolwork is more important than chatting online.

   C They don't understand why she goes on the chatroom every day.

4 What does Alessandra say about chatting to people online?

   A She never tells them about problems.

   B She gives them advice when they need it.

   C She thinks they are very kind.

5 Alessandra thinks that in the future she will

   A try other chatrooms.

   B stop using all chatrooms.

   C continue to use Teen-Age.

3   **Pieter asks his friend Sami to come to his house for dinner. Tick (✓) the two polite responses to the question.**

Pieter: Would you like to come to my house for dinner on Sunday, Sami?

Sami:

1. No, I can't. ☐

2. Thanks, that's a lovely idea. ☐

3. I'm afraid I'm busy then. ☐

4. No, I wouldn't like to. ☐

Feelings, opinions and experiences

1 Put the words into the correct order to make sentences and questions.

1. Japan / been / to / never / have / I / . ...
2. here / she / worked / years / for / has / three / . ...
3. mountain / have / a / climbed / ever / you / ? ....
4. just / mum / have / I / seen / your/ . ...
5. the / started / film / yet / has / ? ....
6. dinner / already / I / finished / have / my / . ...
7. for / we / lived / months / have / here / two / . ...
8. to / wanted / I / him / always / meet / have / ! ....

☑️ Exam task

2 For each question, choose the correct answer.

| HOME | FEATURES | ABOUT ME | CONTACT ME | | SEARCH |

My name's Zack and I'm 14. This summer my dad and I travelled to Tanzania to climb Mount Kilimanjaro, Africa's highest mountain. My dad and I have climbed many mountains in Scotland since I was little, but, at 5,895 metres, Kilimanjaro was higher than anything I'd done before. Planning the trip took months, including a few weeks training in the mountains of Switzerland.

Over 20,000 people climb Kilimanjaro every year. Some do it because the countryside is very interesting, going from rainforest to snow at the top. Our reason was that you can get to the top without ropes and special climbing kit. There are also few storms on the mountain, but we only learnt that later.

Some UK travel companies only take people older than fifteen up Kilimanjaro. I thought this was strange because the youngest person to climb it was only seven. But a company in Tanzania with experience of climbing with kids allowed us to book their trip.

Climbing above 4,000 metres can be difficult because some people get terrible headaches. I was fine, but others in our group were sick, including Dad, so I had to look after him as we got near the top. The other problem was he lost his gloves. His hands got so cold, he couldn't feel them. This was dangerous, so I gave him my socks to keep his hands warm.

It took us six days altogether and it was my best experience ever. I'd do it again tomorrow.

1   Where did Zack and his dad practise before climbing Kilimanjaro?

    A   Scotland

    B   Switzerland

    C   Tanzania

2   Why did Zack and his dad want to climb Kilimanjaro?

    A   Not much equipment is needed.

    B   The countryside is beautiful.

    C   There aren't storms on the mountain.

3   What problem was there with booking the trip?

    A   Not many UK companies offer climbing holidays.

    B   It was hard to book with Tanzanian travel companies.

    C   Some travel companies thought Zack wasn't old enough.

4   What does Zack say about some of the other people in their group?

    A   They were surprised by how cold it was.

    B   They became ill as they climbed the mountain.

    C   They weren't wearing the right clothes for climbing.

5   What is the best title for this article?

    A   A difficult trip for me

    B   My dad's first big climb

    C   Helping my dad on the mountain

---

3 🔊 Track 2 **Listen to the conversations and answer the questions.**

1. When will they go shopping? ....

2. Do the speakers agree with each other? ....

3. Does the man like his new phone? ....

4. What time will they leave? ....

5. Did the woman like the film? ....

6. What do they decide to eat? ....

7. What will the man wear? ....

8. Does the man prefer his laptop or the woman's laptop? ....

> ☑ **Exam tips**
>
> • You have to answer a question or complete a sentence.
> • You will read information about all three answers (A, B and C), but only one is correct.
> • Don't choose an answer just because you see the same words as in the text.

Hobbies and leisure

1 ⟩ **Complete these sentences with the correct word. The first letter of each word is given to help you.**

1. A cinema is a place where people go to watch f ....
2. If you want to see a p .... you can go to a theatre.
3. My hobby is photography. I've just bought a new c ....
4. My younger brother loves c .... and he wants to be a chef when he's older.
5. I'm going out for a m .... tonight, to my favourite restaurant.
6. I'm interested in history. I often go to a m .... to look at things from the past.
7. My friend spends a lot of time on his computer playing v .... games.
8. I play the piano. Do you play a musical i .... ?

2 ⟩ **Read the sentences in italics. Then choose the correct meaning.**

1. *Please try to return books to the correct shelf. Thank you.*
   - **A** Put books back in the correct place.
   - **B** Bring books back at the correct time.

2. *Need to find a room in a hotel? We can book one for you.*
   - **A** We help people who want to work in a hotel.
   - **B** We help people who want to stay in a hotel.

3. *Information about bus and train times at this desk only.*
   - **A** Buy bus and train tickets here.
   - **B** Find out when to catch a bus or train here.

4. *Please pay for maps in cash.*
   - **A** Use coins or notes to buy a map here.
   - **B** Use a bank card to buy a map here.

5. *Computer course for beginners. Starts Monday.*
   - **A** The computer course begins on Monday.
   - **B** The computer course finishes on Monday.

6. *Lost your credit card? Call this number immediately: 970097 86809.*
   - **A** Phone this number if you can't find your credit card.
   - **B** Phone this number if your credit card isn't working.

◎ Get it right!

Look at the sentence below. Then try to correct the mistake.

There are lots of things to see here, and I already saw the Statue of Liberty and the American Museum of Natural History.

3

For each question, choose the correct answer.

Playing the drums

Beth Jones was only eight years old when she first tried playing the drums. This was during a lunchtime music club at school, which she only went to because it was cold and rainy. Also her friends were in the playground playing hockey – a sport that Beth hated. Of all the musical instruments that the teacher had in the music room, the drums were the most interesting to Beth. She thought it was cool that there were many different shapes and sizes of drums, and she wanted to hit them, to see what they sounded like.

Now Beth is thirteen and gives concerts around the country. She also has her own YouTube channel and gets over a million hits a year. What's amazing is that Beth hasn't ever been to a drum lesson. 'You can learn anything on the internet, so I've never felt it was important for me to take classes,' explains Beth.

Giving concerts wasn't easy for Beth at the beginning because usually she only played drums alone in her bedroom when she came home from school. At her first concert, she played in a band with adults. She could feel hundreds of pairs of eyes looking at her, and that made her feel frightened.

So, does Beth enjoy being famous now? 'I didn't plan to be famous,' she says. 'All I want is to show others what I love. I don't think I'm someone special. I just want everyone to have a great time at my concerts.'

1   Why did Beth go to the music club at her school?

    A   She was too ill to play hockey outside.

    B   She wanted something to do one lunchtime.

    C   Her friends were away from school on a sports trip.

2   What is the writer explaining in the first paragraph?

    A   Why Beth chose the drums and not another instrument.

    B   Why the music teacher wanted Beth to try the drums.

    C   Why Beth thought the drums were so hard to play.

3   What does Beth say about drum lessons?

    A   She is sometimes sorry she didn't take lessons.

    B   She thinks lessons can be useful for some people.

    C   She has always thought she doesn't need lessons.

4   What do we learn about Beth's first concert?

    A   It was scary because many people were watching her.

    B   It was easier playing in a band than at home alone.

    C   It was difficult to be in a concert and do her schoolwork.

5   What do we learn about Beth in the final paragraph?

    A   Being a young drummer makes her feel special.

    B   She hopes people enjoy themselves at her concerts.

    C   Her life has changed a lot since she became famous.

Sports and games

1a Put the words for sports and games into the correct part of the table.

chess	exercise	fishing
football	golf	karate	skiing
swimming	tennis

go	play	do
....	....	....
....	....	....
....	....	....
....	....	....

1b Look at the table. Are there any rules about which verb to use with which nouns? Can you add more words for sports or games to the table?

☑ Exam task

2 Read the article about tennis.

Choose the best word (A, B or C) for each space.

Tennis

The English name 'tennis' comes from the French word 'tenez', which means 'to hold'. When the first game of tennis was played hundreds of years ago, people **(1)** .... their hands to hit the ball. Now, of course, we have rackets **(2)** ....

In the **(3)** .... game of tennis, a player **(4)** .... to get four points to win a game, and six games to win a set. In women's tennis, a player wins the match by winning two sets. This is **(5)** .... the same in men's tennis but, in some competitions, men need to win three sets to win a match.

If two people play against each other, it is called a singles match. If there are two players on each side, it is **(6)** .... a doubles match.

1	**A** gave	**B** used	**C** took
2	**A** anymore	**B** else	**C** instead
3	**A** available	**B** ready	**C** modern
4	**A** has	**B** should	**C** must
5	**A** especially	**B** usually	**C** extremely
6	**A** called	**B** known	**C** said

Complete the sentences with the correct alternatives.

1. When I *cycled / was cycling* in the park, I *saw / was seeing* Cristina.
2. I hurt my leg while I *played / was playing* football.
3. I *called / was calling* you at 8 o'clock last night, but you didn't answer. What *did you do / were you doing*?
4. We were so late for the match that they *already played / were already playing* when we arrived.
5. We *played / were playing* tennis when it started raining, so we *stopped / were stopping*.
6. *Did you go / Were you going* skiing when you were in Austria?
7. I *forgot / was forgetting* to bring my badminton racket, but Fay had two so she *lent / was lending* me one.
8. I *met / was meeting* a really interesting man when I *fished / was fishing* yesterday.

Write a few sentences about a sport that you like.

....
....
....
....
....
....
....
....
....
....

☑ *Exam facts*

- In this part, you read a short text – for example from an encyclopedia or article.
- There are six missing words in the text.
- You have to choose the correct word (A, B or C) to complete each space.

Entertainment and media ⟩

1 ⟩ Match the definitions (1–8) to the musical words (a–h).

1. To play this instrument you have to hit it.	**a** practice
2. A group of people who play music together.	**b** opera
3. A person who plays an instrument.	**c** drum
4. Lots of songs together by the same band or artist.	**d** band
5. You need to do this a lot when you learn to play an instrument.	**e** album
6. You touch the black and white parts of this instrument to play it.	**f** record
7. A musical play where people sing the words.	**g** musician
8. People do this with their music so that other people can listen to it.	**h** keyboard

 ☑ **Exam task** ⟩

2 ⟩ For each question, choose the correct answer.

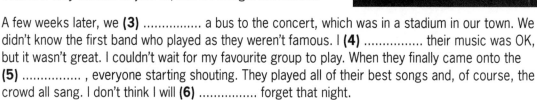

A rock concert

Famous groups don't come to my town very often, so when my brother **(1)** .... me a poster for a concert by my favourite band, I was really **(2)** .... We asked some friends if they wanted to join us, and we bought the tickets.

A few weeks later, we **(3)** .... a bus to the concert, which was in a stadium in our town. We didn't know the first band who played as they weren't famous. I **(4)** .... their music was OK, but it wasn't great. I couldn't wait for my favourite group to play. When they finally came onto the **(5)** .... , everyone starting shouting. They played all of their best songs and, of course, the crowd all sang. I don't think I will **(6)** .... forget that night.

1	**A** took	**B** explained	**C** showed
2	**A** excited	**B** interesting	**C** funny
3	**A** travelled	**B** caught	**C** went
4	**A** want	**B** suppose	**C** hope
5	**A** theatre	**B** curtain	**C** stage
6	**A** still	**B** already	**C** ever

3 Read the suggestions. Choose the TWO correct answers from a, b or c.

1. Why don't we go to a museum at the weekend?
   a I won't do that at all.
   b I'd prefer to go to a concert.
   c OK, that sounds good.

2. Shall we have dinner together on Friday?
   a I'm busy then, but maybe another day?
   b I'm sorry, I'm busy then.
   c I don't think we will, no.

3. Let's watch a film.
   a No, we're not.
   b No, let's do something else.
   c No, not just at the moment.

4. How about going to a concert on Sunday?
   a Yes, I'd love to.
   b Yes, that's right.
   c Yes, that's a great idea.

5. Why don't you ask Maya to come to the opera?
   a I don't think she likes opera.
   b Because I don't like opera.
   c I might do that!

6. Shall we listen to some music?
   a Maybe later?
   b Yeah, lovely!
   c We shall not.

7. I'll take a photo, shall I?
   a No, don't worry.
   b Yes, you will.
   c No, I'll do it.

8. Let's go dancing at the weekend.
   a Sure, why not?
   b Yes, let's do.
   c That's not a bad idea!

☑ **Exam tips**

- Quickly read the text before you choose your answers.
- Try each word (A, B and C) in the space before you choose the correct answer.
- Read the whole sentence carefully when you choose an answer.

Transport

1a Complete the table with the comparative and superlative forms of the adjectives.

adjective	comparative	superlative
big	....	....
bad	....	....
fast	....	....
dirty	....	....
modern	....	....
healthy	....	....
popular	....	....
crowded	....	....

1b Complete each sentence with a word from Exercise 1a.

1. The traffic is .... during the week than at weekends because everyone is going to work.
2. Wow! I thought my car needed a wash, but yours is even .... than mine!
3. The trains in this city are the .... I've even been on. There are so many people on them!
4. I get home later in the evening now that I walk, but it's .... for me than driving.
5. There's a lot of space in this car – it's .... than the one you had before.
6. In cities which have a river, boats are quite a .... way to get around.
7. A hundred years ago, the .... car in the world could only travel at 136 km/h.
8. We have a lovely .... railway station now – much better than the old one.

☑ **Exam task**

2 For each question, choose the correct answer.

Better ways to travel

Millions of us use our cars every day to get to work, college or school. Travelling by car is fast and comfortable, but not **(1)** .... for the world around us. So what should we do? One possibility is to **(2)** .... car journeys. If you have neighbours who need to travel to the same **(3)** .... as you, why not go together in one car? Two or three people travelling together is a more intelligent idea than two or three cars **(4)** .... the same journey with only one person in each car.

Of course, cars are not the only way to travel. It's usually possible to travel by bus, tram or train, **(5)** .... in a town or city. And if your journey is short, what about walking or going by bike? You'll get fit and **(6)** .... money too!

1	**A** good	**B** well	**C** better
2	**A** add	**B** share	**C** join
3	**A** trip	**B** map	**C** place
4	**A** bringing	**B** making	**C** getting
5	**A** absolutely	**B** really	**C** especially
6	**A** save	**B** hold	**C** keep

3a Read the predictions about the future. Look at the <u>underlined</u> phrases and number them 1–5 (1 = most likely to happen, 5 = least likely to happen).

a <u>I think</u> plane journeys will be shorter in the future. ....

b <u>It's possible</u> that / <u>Maybe</u> we'll all have flying cars in the future. ....

c <u>I'm very sure</u> / <u>I'm certain</u> that our journeys to work will be shorter because trains are getting faster. ....

d <u>I'm not sure</u> if we'll still travel by train a hundred years from now. ....

e <u>I'm sure</u> we won't use petrol in our cars for much longer. ....

3b Write five sentences about what you think will happen to transport in the future. Use the phrases from Exercise 3a.

1. ....

2. ....

3. ....

4. ....

5. ....

 **Get it right!**

Look at the sentences below and choose the correct one.

The most thing I like about it is the camera.

The thing I like most about it is the camera.

Daily life

1 ⟩ Complete the gaps in the text with the correct form of the verbs in the box.

be	close	have	need
take	walk	want	work

Every day I wake up at 8 a.m., and **(1)** .... a bus into town. I eat breakfast at a café, and then **(2)** .... to my family's shop. I **(3)** .... in the shop, helping my father. He **(4)** .... the manager of the shop. We **(5)** .... lunch at about 12:30 p.m. and Dad **(6)** .... the shop at 5 p.m. I like my job, and I know Dad **(7)** .... me, but in the future I **(8)** .... to travel, so I'm saving money to pay for that.

☑️ Exam task

2 ⟩ For each question, write the correct answer. Write ONE word for each gap.
Example: **0** *in*

●●●   <u>Reply</u>   <u>Forward</u>

Hi Jenni,
How are you? Is your new life **(0)** .... Canada going well? And **(1)** .... is your university course like? Have you made new friends? **(2)** .... you think you might come back for a visit soon?
Clara

●●●   <u>Reply</u>   <u>Forward</u>

Hi Clara,
I'm fine, thanks. I've been here for a month now. It was quite difficult for the first few weeks **(3)** .... I didn't know anyone, but now I know more people, I'm starting **(4)** .... enjoy myself. I'm sure that I **(5)** .... come home for a few weeks before the end of **(6)** .... year, so see you in a few months.
Keep writing to me!
Jenni

3a Complete Jenni's next email to Clara with the correct alternatives.

Reply   Forward

Hi Clara,
You asked me **(1)** *that / what* I do every day. Well, I get up early **(2)** *because / so* my
first class is **(3)** *at / in* 8 a.m. I drive to the university. **(4)** *After / When* I'm not in class,
I usually go to the library to study, and I meet friends **(5)** *with / for* lunch. In the evenings,
(6) *there / here* are concerts and sometimes parties. I go to some of **(7)** *they / them* with
my friends, **(8)** *but / as* I also study a lot.
Jenni

3b Imagine that a friend has asked you what you do each day. Write an email to them about your typical day.

....
....
....
....
....
....
....
....
....

☑ *Exam facts*

- In this part, you read one or two short texts. These are usually email messages.
- There are six missing words in the text(s).
- You have to write the six missing words.

Social interaction

1 ⟩ **Complete the sentences with the correct alternatives.**

1. I *would / may* see him later, but I'm not sure.
2. *May / Can* you swim a kilometre?
3. Do you think I *should / shall* invite him?
4. I *would / might* go to the party if I'm not too tired.
5. *Could / Would* you like to come to dinner tomorrow?
6. My brother *shouldn't / couldn't* walk until he was nearly two!
7. *Shall / Would* I help you get lunch ready?
8. Excuse me – you *mustn't / might not* smoke in here!

2a ⟩ **Complete the conversation with the correct form of the verbs in brackets.**

Gleb: Hi, Jan. I **(1)** .... (not / see) you for ages! What **(2)** .... (you / do) here?

Jan: I **(3)** .... (visit) my sister. She **(4)** .... (live) here for about three months.

Gleb: Oh, great! And **(5)** .... (you / still / study) at college?

Jan: Yes, but not maths. I **(6)** .... (do) business now. What about you?

Gleb: I **(7)** .... (work) in an office at the moment, but I **(8)** .... (want) to go travelling next year.

Jan: Well, good luck with that. It was nice to see you, Gleb!

2b ⟩ **Write a few sentences about your plans for the weekend.**

....
....
....
....
....
....
....
....
....
....

☑ Exam task

For each question, write the correct answer. Write ONE word for each gap.

Example: **0** *am / 'm*

● ● ●   <u>Reply</u>   <u>Forward</u>

Hi Kris,
I **(0)** .... going cycling with my brother next Sunday.
Would you like **(1)** .... come? Don't worry if you don't
have a good bike – we've got one you can borrow. We'll take a
picnic, so we won't need to eat in a café.
Let **(2)** .... know if you want to come.
Ali

● ● ●   <u>Reply</u>   <u>Forward</u>

Hi Ali,
That's **(3)** .... great idea. Thanks very much **(4)** .... offering to lend me a bike,
but I got a new one few weeks ago. I'll bring lunch and something to drink. **(5)** ....
there anything else that I should bring? Also, **(6)** .... time do you think we'll be
home? I'm going out in the evening.
Kris

☑ Exam tips

- Quickly read the text(s) before you write the missing words.
- Look at the words that come before and after the space and think about what kind of word you need to write – for example, a noun, verb, preposition, etc.
- Only write one word in each space.
- When you finish, read the text(s) again to make sure they make sense.

Travel and holidays

1   **Complete the text with the correct form of the verbs in brackets.**

Last year, I **(1)** .... (go) on holiday to France. We **(2)** .... (drive) there, which took a long time, but it **(3)** .... (be) good because we **(4)** .... (see) a lot of beautiful countryside on the way. We stayed in a lovely house which **(5)** .... (have) a really big swimming pool. Every day we **(6)** .... (get) up late and **(7)** .... (spend) all day in the sun. We **(8)** .... (eat) fantastic food too. I would like to go to the same place again next year.

☑ Exam task

2   **For each question, write the correct answer. Write ONE word for each gap.**

Example: **0** *at*

```
● ● ●                                            Reply      Forward
```

Hi Mum and Dad,
I hope everything's OK **(0)** .... home. I arrived in New Zealand yesterday. On the plane, I sat next **(1)** .... a really nice woman who told me about **(2)** .... of interesting places I could visit while I'm here. And I've found a place to stay **(3)** .... isn't too expensive. I'm going to be in New Zealand for nearly **(4)** .... month, and then I'm going to fly to **(5)** .... USA.
Dad, did you ask your friend Patricia in San Francisco **(6)** .... it's OK for me to stay with her next month?
I'll write again soon.
Sonia

3 **Put the words in the correct order to make questions and sentences about holiday plans.**

1. year / you / are / this / where / holiday / on / going / ?

....

2. to / the / we / be / at / by / airport / ten / need / .

....

3. year / like / to / next / to / Germany / would / I / go / .

....

4. airport / are / how / the / you / to / getting / ?

....

5. to / family / I / China / going / with / am / my / .

....

6. you / long / will / how / there / stay / ?

....

7. small / a / we / hotel / to / are / stay / in / going / .

....

8. by / you / yourself / going / are / travelling / ?

....

⊙ Get it right!

Look at the sentence below. Then try to correct the mistake.

Now I write a postcard to you and then I'm going to have lunch at the new restaurant on the beach.

Health and exercise

1 Read the email and the reply. Complete the reply with the correct alternatives.

● ● ●   **Reply**   **Forward**

Dear Richard,
I would like to join the gym you go to. Where is it? Which activities does it offer? Can I go
there with you soon?
Ash

● ● ●   **Reply**   **Forward**

Dear Ash,
The gym **(1)** *is / am* on Station Road. I usually **(2)** *taking / take* exercise classes there,
(3) *but / so* yesterday I **(4)** *use / used* the pool. There **(5)** *are / is* exercise machines too.
(6) *I'm going / I go* there tomorrow. Why **(7)** *aren't you coming / don't you come* with me?
See you soon.
Richard

2a Complete the tips about writing emails with the correct alternatives.

When you write an email to a friend, start the email with **(1)** *Dear / Fair* or **(2)** *Hey / Hi*, and
then your friend's **(3)** *title / name*.
To finish your message you can write **(4)** *'best / good* wishes' or 'see you **(5)** *soon / quickly'*.

2b Write a few sentences about your favourite kind of exercise.

....
....
....
....
....
....
....
....

☑ Exam facts

- In this part, you read a short text asking you for three pieces of information.
- The text may be a message or some notes.
- You have to write the three pieces of information in a short message.

3 Your English friend Jo goes running every day. You want to go running with Jo.
Write an email to Jo:

- say when you want to run with Jo
- ask what time Jo goes running
- offer to show Jo a nice place to go running.

Write **25 words** or more.

....
....
....
....
....
....
....
....
....
....

Personal identification

1 Match the definitions (1–6) with the family words (a–f).

1. your mother's brother	**a** grandmother
2. your aunt's son	**b** cousin
3. your father's mother	**c** granddaughter
4. your son's daughter	**d** father
5. your sister's son	**e** nephew
6. your grandfather's son	**f** uncle

2 Complete the conversation with the information from the boxes (a–d).

a 0648 546824.

b The fifth of October, 2000.

c Elsa Merton. That's M-E-R-T-O-N.

d 116, Greenwood Road.

Librarian: You can join the library, but I need some information first. Can you tell me your full name, please?

Elsa: (1) ....

Librarian: Thank you. And where do you live, Elsa?

Elsa: (2) ....

Librarian: That's fine. Now – what's your date of birth?

Elsa: (3) ....

Librarian: OK. And finally, what's your phone number?

Elsa: (4) ....

Librarian: Thank you, Elsa. Here's your card and your book. Now I'll show you around the library.

Read the email from your English friend Maxi.

3

● ● ●   <u>Reply</u>   <u>Forward</u>

I've received a wedding invitation from your brother. It's so nice of him! Can you suggest a place in your city where I can stay? What do people usually wear to weddings in your country? What can I buy them for a present?
Maxi

Write an email to Maxi and answer the questions.

Write **25 words** or more.

....
....
....
....
....
....
....
....
....
....

✓ **Exam tips**

- Read the instructions carefully to find out what you need to write.
- You must write all three pieces of information.
- When you finish your message, check your spelling and grammar.

Entertainment and media

1 ▶ Complete the sentences with the words in the box.

actor	channel	exhibition	fan
movie	screen	stage	video games

1. If you don't like the TV programme, change the ....
2. My friend is a big .... of that group. She goes to all their concerts.
3. I love playing .... online with my friends.
4. I'm going to that photography .... at the museum tomorrow.
5. Let's see that film. Your favourite .... is in it.
6. The .... at that new cinema is really big.
7. I didn't have a good seat at the theatre. I was a long way from the ....
8. Another word for a film is a ....

2 ▶ Add the punctuation (question marks, full stops, capital letters and apostrophes) to the sentences.

1. Id like to go to that concert

....

2. are you going to the party tonight

....

3. my friend sara is going to be in a show

....

4. this isnt carlas guitar

....

5. ive never been to the opera

....

6. i dont like that artist

....

7. i think well need to buy a ticket

....

8. do you know where i live

....

 **Get it right!**

Look at the sentence below. Then try to correct the mistake.

I'm having a day off next week I would like to come to visit you.

3 Your English friend Charlie has invited you to the cinema tomorrow, but you can't go.

Write an email to Charlie:

- tell Charlie that you are sorry
- explain why you can't go
- say which day you can go instead.

Write **25 words** or more.

....
....
....
....
....
....
....
....
....
....

Food and drink

1a **Read the sentences about working in a restaurant. Choose the best word (A, B or C) for each space.**

1. The waiter speaks to each customer and writes their .... in a notebook.
   A order   **B** menu   **C** sign

2. Sometimes the waiter needs to .... to customers what is in the dishes.
   A understand   **B** decide   **C** explain

3. The chef tries to .... the food as quickly as possible.
   A prepare   **B** improve   **C** cover

4. When the food is ready, the waiter .... it to the customers.
   A leaves   **B** serves   **C** puts

5. When the customers finish their meal, they ask the waiter for their ....
   A price   **B** bill   **C** purse

1b **Read the phrases below and decide who is speaking. Write W (waiter) or C (customer).**

1. Excuse me, could I have some water, please? ....

2. That dessert comes with cream or ice cream. Which would you prefer? ....

3. My food is delicious. Is yours nice too? ....

4. I think I'm going to have a dessert. They're really good here. ....

5. Are you ready to order now? ....

6. Good evening. A table for two, please. ....

7. Shall I take your plates now? ....

8. I'd like an extra-large cheese and tomato pizza with chips, please. ....

2 **Look at the three pictures and read the story. Which picture does each sentence describe?**

  A   B   C

1. The boys ate everything on the table and when they were finished, they felt really full!   ....

2. It was Johann's birthday, so he and his friends went to their favourite restaurant.   ....

3. They were all very hungry, so they ordered the largest pizzas on the menu.   ....

Look at the three pictures. Write the story shown in the pictures. Write 35 words or more.

....

....

....

....

....

....

....

....

☑ **Exam facts**

- In this part, you see three pictures.
- You have to write the story shown in the three pictures.
- Your story should be 35 words or more.

Clothes

1a Read the descriptions of some words for clothes. What is the word for each one? The first letter is given to you. There is one space for each letter in the word.

1. You wear these on your hands.   g _ _ _ _ _
2. You wear this around your neck on a cold day.   s _ _ _ _
3. You wear this in summer. It's cooler than a sweater.   T - _ _ _ _ _
4. These are a type of trousers.   j _ _ _ _
5. These are shoes you can wear for doing sports.   t _ _ _ _ _ _ _
6. You wear this on your head.   c _ _
7. You wear this over your shirt, like a coat.   j _ _ _ _ _

1b Complete the sentences with the correct alternatives.

1. Remy, is this scarf *you / your / yours*?
2. *What / Who / Which* does this jumper belong to?
3. My cousin is only two, but she can already dress *herself / itself / yourself*.
4. I've brought a spare swimming costume because I thought *someone / anyone / no one* might forget theirs.
5. I can't find my belt. Do you have *this / one / it* I can borrow?
6. I need to buy some ties for work. I don't have *many / much / more*.

2 Look at these words and expressions from a story. Sort the words into three groups.

Finally	One day	Then	Last week
After that	In the end	Suddenly	On Saturday morning

1 Beginning of the story	2 Middle of the story	3 End of the story
....	....	....
....	....	....
....	....	....

☑ *Exam task*

Look at the three pictures. Write the story shown in the pictures. Write 35 words or more.

....
....
....
....
....
....
....
....

☑ *Exam tips*

- You don't get extra marks for writing a very long story.
- You only need to describe what's happening in the three pictures.
- It's possible to use direct speech in your story.
- When you have finished your story, read it again to check spelling and grammar.

The weather

1 Read the descriptions of some words about the weather. For each description, choose the correct word from the box.

storm	clouds	fog	rain	ice	dry	sunny

1. These are white, grey or black, and you can see them in the sky. ....
2. When the weather is very cold, water changes to this. ....
3. During one of these, you may hear thunder. ....
4. This is the opposite of wet. ....
5. When you can see the sun in the sky, we say the weather is this. ....
6. In this weather, it's difficult to see where you are going. ....
7. This is water that falls from the sky. ....

2a Match the comments about the weather (1–6) to the replies (a–f).

1. It's going to be hot today.
2. The weather was great at the weekend.
3. Do you think it'll rain later?
4. What's the weather like where you live?
5. I love the snow!
6. Did you hear the thunderstorm last night?

a Me too. It's fun to play in.
b Really? Oh, I'll change my clothes then.
c No. I was asleep.
d But it's so different today!
e Yes, take your umbrella.
f It's warm and sunny here, as usual.

2b Write a few sentences about the weather yesterday.

....
....
....
....
....
....
....
....
....
....
....
....

 **Exam task**

3

Look at the three pictures. Write the story shown in the pictures. Write 35 words or more.

....

....

....

....

....

....

....

....

Get it right!

Look at the sentences below. Which one is correct?

It was a beautiful sun day.

It was a beautiful sunny day.

Services and places

1 Match the questions (1–10) to the answers (a–j).

1. When shall we meet?	**a** At 8:30 a.m. every day.
2. What time does the next train leave?	**b** At 6:15 p.m., outside the cinema.
3. When is your sister's birthday?	**c** At twenty to eight, on platform three.
4. What time does the post office open?	**d** In 2009. We were in the same class at school.
5. When is your doctor's appointment?	**e** Saturday. I love the weekend!
6. How long have you lived in Sydney?	**f** Next Wednesday at 1:15 p.m.
7. When do you play hockey?	**g** On the 22nd of September.
8. Excuse me, what's the time please?	**h** On Tuesdays, in the sports centre.
9. When did you meet your best friend?	**i** Since 2014.
10. What's your favourite day of the week?	**j** It's ten o'clock.

☑ *Exam task*

2 🔊 Track 3

For each question, choose the correct answer.

1 Where is the post office?

A ☐

B ☐

C ☐

2 What does the man order?

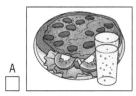
A ☐

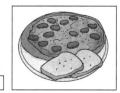
B ☐

C ☐

3 How much does the man spend?

A ☐

B ☐

C ☐

4 Where are the girls going today?

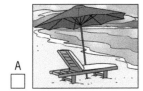

A ☐

B ☐

C ☐

5 When is the woman going to the dentist?

A ☐

B ☐

C ☐

3 Match the words in the box to the sentences and questions.

cinema	dentist	hotel	library	museum	restaurant
sports centre	theatre		tourist information centre		train station

1. The paintings were discovered in Italy in 1843. ....

2. Excuse me, what time does the play finish? ....

3. Can I have a return ticket to Bradford, please? ....

4. You are in room 321, on the third floor. Here is the key. Enjoy your stay. ....

5. I'll have a chicken salad, please. ....

6. Would you like a map of the city? ....

7. Good morning. I've got an appointment at 4:30. ....

8. What time does the aerobics class start? ....

9. Let's buy tickets for the new James Bond film now! ....

10. Can I borrow these books, please? ....

☑ **Exam facts**

- In this part, you listen to five short conversations.
- There are five questions with three pictures.
- You have to choose the right picture.

Shopping and numbers

1 Complete the sentences with the numbers in the box.

eight	fifteen	seven	sixty	twelve	twenty-six	two hundred	thousand

1. There are .... days in a week.

2. When it's 11:45, it is also a quarter to ....

3. There are a .... metres in a kilometre.

4. I'm 24 and my sister is 16. She's .... years younger than me.

5. There are .... seconds in a minute.

6. Paula lives at 16 Brick Lane and her friend lives next door at number ....

7. There are .... letters in the English alphabet.

8. Our house was built in 1793. It's over .... years old.

☑ Exam task

🔊 Track 4

2

For each question, choose the correct answer.

1 Which bus goes to the supermarket?

A

B

C

2 What time does the shop close?

A

B

C

3 Which T-shirt does the woman buy?

A

B

C

4 What time does the bookshop close on Saturday?

A ☐

B ☐

C ☐

5 What did the man buy?

A ☐

B ☐

C ☐

3 Read the descriptions and complete the words. The first letter is given to you. There is one space for each letter in the word.

1. If you haven't got any cash you will need to pay with this. c _ _ _ _ _   c _ _ _
2. When you buy something the shop assistant will give you this. r _ _ _ _ _ _
3. This is a shop with many floors where you can buy lots of different things. d _ _ _ _ _ _ _ _ _
   s _ _ _ _
4. These are people who buy things in a shop. c _ _ _ _ _ _ _ _
5. There are 100 pennies in one of these. p _ _ _ _
6. You can buy food and other things in this shop. s _ _ _ _ _ _ _ _ _ _
7. You might do this before you buy new clothes. t _ _ (them) _ _
8. If you like reading, you might go to this shop. b _ _ _ _ _ _ _
9. Shoppers in the USA spend these. d _ _ _ _ _ _
10. When you are shopping you can ask this person for help. a _ _ _ _ _ _ _ _

☑ **Exam tips**

- Read the questions very carefully. <u>Underline</u> the most important words in the question.
- The people will talk about what you can see in all three pictures, but only one is right.
- The first time you listen, choose your answers. The second time you listen, check that your answers are right.

Education and study

1

Choose the correct alternative in each sentence.

1. What time *did / does* the class finish last week?
2. Fran is always tired on Saturdays so she *got up / gets up* late.
3. *Was / Does* your mum work in a bank?
4. Max *bought / is going to buy* a new mobile phone later.
5. Kate *sends / sent* me an email two days ago.
6. *Did you / Are you going to* visit your grandmother tomorrow?
7. I sometimes *meet / am going to meet* my friends at the beach.
8. *Is / Was* Ben wearing a hat at the party last night?
9. I think *I'll go / I went* shopping tomorrow.
10. Matt usually walks home but this afternoon he is going to *ride / rides* his bike.

☑ Exam task

2

🔊 Track 5

For each question, choose the correct answer.

1 What is the boy's favourite subject?

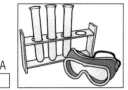
A

B

C

2 Where does the girl put the dictionary?

A

B

C

3 What does the boy lend the girl?

A

B

C

4 What time does the TV programme start?

A

B

C

5 Where does the medical student have lessons?

A

B

C

3 **Read about Teresa's day, then choose the correct alternative.**

> Hello. My name's Teresa. I am a teacher in a secondary school. I usually wake up at 7:30, have a shower and get dressed. Then I have toast for breakfast. I always listen to the news on the radio while I am having breakfast. I leave the house at 8:30 and I cycle to work. I start at 9:00 and school finishes at 4:15. After work, I often go to the pool. When I get home, I make dinner, and eat it in the living room while I watch TV. After dinner I do the washing up, walk my dog on the beach and sometimes phone my friends. I usually go to bed at 10:30. I love reading travel magazines and always look at them before I go to sleep.

1. Teresa works in a *bank / school*.
2. She has *cereal / toast* for breakfast.
3. While she is having breakfast, she listens to *music / the news*.
4. Teresa goes to work by *bike / car*.
5. She starts work at *eight thirty / nine o'clock*.
6. After work, she often *shops / swims*.
7. She watches TV while she is *cooking / eating*.
8. She eats dinner in the *living room / kitchen*.
9. She walks her dog *in the park / on the beach*.
10. She usually reads *emails / magazines* before she goes to sleep.

 *Get it right!*

Look at the sentences below and choose the correct one.

Next week, I'm going to an interesting place near your town.

Next week, I go to an interesting place near your town.

Making plans

1a Complete the sentences with the words in the box.

| autumn | birthday | century | clock | diary | evening | weekly | yesterday |

1. Today is Wednesday, so .... was Tuesday.
2. The big .... on the wall in my office says it's 5:15 p.m.
3. If you have a meeting every Monday, it's a .... meeting.
4. There are one hundred years in a ....
5. The book where people write their appointments is called a ....
6. .... is the season when the leaves fall from the trees.
7. People usually give you presents on your ....
8. The time between the afternoon and the night is called the ....

1b Complete the table with the words and phrases in the box.

every day	Friday morning	half past three	January
last year	Mondays	the afternoon	the moment
the weekend	tomorrow	2013	15th May

at	in	on	no preposition
....	....	....	....
....	....	....	....
....	....	....	....

 Exam task

2 ◀») Track 6

For each question, write the correct answer in the gap.

Write one word or a number or a date or a time.
You will hear a woman talking about renting a boat for a holiday.

Riverboat Holidays

Name of boat: Moonlight

Boat is for: **(1)** between two and .... people

Dates available this year: 1st–31st **(2)** ....

Total cost: **(3)** £ .... per week

Must bring: **(4)** ....

Phone number to book: **(5)** ....

3 Read the conversation. Choose the best word for each space, a, b or c.

Mario: Hello Tanya. Where are you **(1)** …. to go on holiday this year?

Tanya: I **(2)** …. going to go to Tenerife in August.

Mario: That sounds fun! Will it be hot?

Tanya: Yes, it **(3)** …. . I've bought a new hat and some sunglasses.

Mario: Really? Who **(4)** …. you going to go with?

Tanya: With my friends Lara and Michelle.

Mario: My sister went to Tenerife last year. She said that the beaches are amazing.

Tanya: I know. But we **(5)** …. have a lot of free time to explore the island!

Mario: Why not? What are you going to do?

Tanya: We **(6)** …. going to study Spanish in a language school.

Mario: That sounds fun. Are you going **(7)** …. lessons every day?

Tanya: Yes, we are.

Mario: Do you think you **(8)** …. be in the same class as your friends?

Tanya: No, we **(9)** …. be, because my friends speak better Spanish than me.

Mario: **(10)** …. you send me a postcard?

Tanya: Yes, of course! What's your address?

1. **a** going   **b** doing   **c** will

2. **a** 'm   **b** 's   **c** 'll

3. **a** going   **b** is   **c** will

4. **a** is   **b** are   **c** will

5. **a** am   **b** will   **c** won't

6. **a** 'm   **b** 're   **c** 'll

7. **a** has   **b** have   **c** to have

8. **a** are   **b** will   **c** is

9. **a** aren't   **b** will   **c** won't

10. **a** Will   **b** Going to   **c** Are

☑ **Exam facts**

- In this part, you listen to one person speaking.
- There are some notes with five spaces for you to complete.
- You have to write a word, a number, a date or a time in each space.

> ## Health, medicine and exercise

1 **Read the descriptions and complete the words. The first letter is given to you. There is one space for each letter in the word.**

1. If you have a problem with this, you go to the dentist. t _ _ _ _
2. You use these to see. e _ _ _
3. This might be curly or straight. h _ _ _
4. You wear shoes on these. f _ _ _
5. Some animals have got a big one of these, for example humans and dolphins. b _ _ _ _
6. This is between your head and your body. n _ _ _
7. You have ten of these on your hands. f _ _ _ _ _ _
8. This moves your blood around your body. h _ _ _ _
9. If you eat a lot of cake, you might have a pain here. s _ _ _ _ _ _
10. Some people write with their left one of these. h _ _ _

> ☑ **Exam task**

2 🔊 Track 7

For each question, write the correct answer in the gap.
Write one word or a number or a date or a time.
You will hear a woman talking about a medical centre.

Medical centre

Address: Park Street

Centre is next to: the **(1)** ....

Doctor's name: Dr **(2)** ....

Doctor speaks: English and **(3)** ....

Closes every Tuesday at: **(4)** .... p.m.

Hospital phone number: **(5)** ....

3 Read the conversations. Choose the correct modal verb.

1. I've got toothache.

You *might / should* go to the dentist!

2. Chris has fallen off his motorbike and now his arm hurts.

It *might / should* be broken so he *might not / shouldn't* move.

3. Emma fell over when she was running and has hurt her ankle.

I think she *might / should* put a bandage on it.

4. I've got a headache.

You *might / should* lie down in your bedroom and take this medicine.

5. Can you help me? I've cut my hand on a rock.

There is a lot of blood so you *might / should* see a doctor.

6. Lucy is very hot.

She *might not / shouldn't* go to school today because she *might / should* have a temperature.

7. I'm really tired and I don't feel well.

You *might / should* go to bed. You will feel better tomorrow.

8. Mum, I feel sick. My stomach hurts.

You *might not / shouldn't* eat any more sweets, Jeremy. And take some medicine.

☑ **Exam tips**

- Before you listen, read the form carefully.
- Think about what kind of information you need to write for each question – for example, a day, time, name, phone number, etc.
- If the word is the name of person or a place, the speaker will spell it. The other words will be vocabulary we use in everyday life.

Dates and services

1a **Match the numbers to the words.**

1st	fifth
2nd	first
3rd	fourteenth
4th	fourth
5th	ninth
9th	second
12th	third
13th	thirteenth
14th	thirty-first
20th	twelfth
25th	twentieth
31st	twenty-fifth

1b **Complete the sentences with the words from Exercise 1a.**

1. The Listening paper is the .... part of the exam.

2. March is the .... month of the year.

3. *E* is the .... letter of the alphabet.

4. December is the .... month of the year.

5. Halloween is on the .... of October.

6. *M* is the .... letter of the alphabet.

7. Christmas Day is on the .... of December.

8. September is the .... month of the year.

9. Valentine's Day is on the .... of February.

10. April is the .... month of the year.

11. *T* is the .... letter of the alphabet.

12. New Year's Day is on the .... of January.

 Get it right!

Look at the sentences below and choose the correct one.

It is very important to me because I will go to New Zealand tomorrow.

It is very important to me because I am going to New Zealand tomorrow.

☑ Exam task

2

🔊 Track 8

For each question, write the correct answer in the gap.
Write one word or a number or a date or a time.
You will hear a teacher talking about photography lessons.

<u>Photography course</u>
Start: 3rd October
Day of course during October: **(1)** ....
Cost: **(2)** £ ....
Month when college is closed: **(3)** ....
College office closes in the evening at: **(4)** ....
Address: **(5)** 59 .... Street

3 **Choose the correct response to each question, a, b or c.**

1. What time does the museum close at the weekend?
    a It opens on Saturdays. **b** At half past seven. **c** Yes, every week.

2. When is your birthday?
    a It's at five o'clock. **b** It's in 1995. **c** It's on the 3rd of May.

3. When is your favourite programme on TV?
    a On the 6th December. **b** On Wednesday evenings. **c** I saw it last September.

4. Do you have swimming lessons on Tuesdays?
    a No, last week. **b** On Mondays. **c** Yes, from seven to eight in the evening.

5. When are you going on holiday?
    a On the 13th of October. **b** Yesterday, with my parents. **c** On Tuesdays from 7 p.m. to 9 p.m.

6. What time do you get up?
    a In the morning. **b** At a quarter past seven on weekdays. **c** It's nine o'clock in the morning.

7. When will the new video game be on sale?
    a I play it every week. **b** Last week. It was great. **c** In the spring, I think.

8. Is the sports centre open on Sundays?
    a Yes, it opens at 9 a.m. **b** It's open every day from Monday to Saturday. **c** No, it closes at 5 p.m.

Leisure time

1

Match the questions (1–6) to the answers (a–f). Then underline the answer word(s).

1. How much did you pay for that video game, Chris? ....
2. Was it sunny in France last week, Jane? ....
3. When do you have dance lessons, Alex? ....
4. What time does the picnic start on Sunday? ....
5. When are you going to the *One Star* concert in London? ....
6. Where did Bella learn English? ....

a They are playing for three nights, but my ticket's for the 25th of September.

b The full price is £15, but my brother works in the computer shop and he gets a discount, so I only paid £12!

c At about 12.00, but I'm meeting Felix at the station at 11:30 and we're going together.

d No, it wasn't. It was cloudy, but it didn't rain!

e Every Friday. Do you want to come next week?

f She lived in London for two years when she was twenty.

☑ Exam task

2

◀)) Track 9

For each question, choose the correct answer. You will hear Jack talking to his friend Martin about music.

1 What is the name of Martin's music teacher?

A Harry

B Peter

C Steve

2 Martin has music lessons on

A Tuesdays.

B Thursdays.

C Saturdays.

3 How long does Martin practise at the weekend?

A 1 hour

B 2 hours

C 3 hours

4 Martin likes the music festival because

A tickets are free.

B the bands are local.

C there are lots of people there.

5 Jack will arrive at the music festival

A at 6:15.

B at 7:00.

C at 7:45.

3a Complete the table with the words in the box.

the beach	a bike	a camera	the cinema	cooking
a fishing rod	go to a festival	go to a restaurant		have a barbecue
have a picnic	a mobile phone		a museum	painting
the park	reading	taking photos		

Favourite things	Hobbies	Places to go	Things to do at the weekend
....	....	....	....
....	....	....	....
....	....	....	....
....	....	....	....

3b Answer the questions about yourself.

1. What do you do in your free time?

....

2. Can you play an instrument?

....

3. What is your favourite thing?

....

4. Where do you usually meet your friends?

....

5. How often do you go the cinema?

....

6. What did you do yesterday afternoon?

....

7. What are you going to do at the weekend?

....

8. Have you ever been to a music festival?

....

☑ **Exam facts**

- In this part, you listen to a conversation between two people.
- There are five questions and you have to choose the right answer (A, B or C).
- The answers come from both speakers. One of the speakers can give three or four of the answers.

Social media and technology

1

Put the letters in the right order to make words. Then complete the sentences.

1. I usually .... games onto my laptop computer to practise my English. (dwondaol)

2. I use my .... to call my friends, take photos and send messages. (emboil npohe)

3. You can find out about lots of things on the .... (ietrentn)

4. I often play .... in my spare time. (voied gsmae)

5. My favourite band have got an amazing .... with interesting facts and information on it. (wbe pega)

6. My sister loves taking photos with her .... (dtiliga cmraea)

7. Some people spend many hours chatting to friends .... (oinnel)

8. Q is the first letter on most .... (ekybardos)

9. You can use a .... to open and close documents on your computer. (mesuo)

10. I send lots of .... every day at work. (ealims)

 Exam task

2

 Track 10

For each question, choose the correct answer. You will hear Lisa talking to her friend Robert about computers.

1 Where did Lisa buy her laptop?

  A Bridge Street

  B Green Street

  C High Street

2 The most useful website Robert has seen is

  A buy-a-computer.com

  B parks-computers.com

  C new-laptop.com

3 Lisa's new laptop weighs

  A one kilogramme.

  B 1.5 kilogrammes.

  C two kilogrammes.

4 How much did Lisa pay for her laptop?

  A £579

  B £699

  C £849

5 Why will Robert buy a new laptop?

  A to talk to his brother

  B to shop online

  C to study

3 | **Rewrite the sentences in the past or present passive.**

1. Martin Cooper invented the first mobile phone in 1973.

....

2. Lots of people watch videos on the internet.

....

3. My brother didn't write that email.

....

4. People often read news articles online.

....

5. Tim Berners-Lee created the first website in 1991.

....

6. Young people usually play video games at home.

....

7. The teacher showed the students some useful websites.

....

☑ **Exam tips**

- You have to answer a question or complete a sentence.
- You will hear information about all three answers, but only one is right.
- Look at the questions to see who will give the answer.

Travel and holidays

1 Complete the sentences with the words in the box. There are some words that you do not need to use.

article	bill	comics	diary	diploma
form	magazines	menu	newspaper	passport
postcard	project	textbook	ticket	

1. My little brother loves reading ....

2. We haven't finished all the exercises in our English .... yet.

3. Great! The .... in this restaurant is in English!

4. Lots of people read fashion ....

5. I usually read the .... on the train in the morning.

6. My sister writes in her .... every day.

7. Sandra, you need to get a new .... to travel to New Zealand.

8. I always send my parents a .... when I'm on holiday.

9. You must keep your .... for the return journey.

10. I read an interesting .... about sport on the internet.

---

2 **Exam task**

◀⑴ Track 11

For each question, choose the correct answer.
You will hear James talking to his friend Susan about his holiday.

1 How long is James's holiday?

  A one week

  B two weeks

  C three weeks

2 Where is James flying to first?

  A Manchester

  B Miami

  C Paris

3 Where did Susan go in January?

  A Canada

  B Mexico

  C the USA

4 How does James feel about the flight to Miami?

  A It will be too long.

  B He will feel tired after it.

  C He will use the time to sleep.

5 Where at the airport will Susan meet James?

  A in the car park

  B in the arrivals hall

  C in the bus station

3a

Match 1–10 with a–j.

1.	I'm	**a**	'm flying to Mallorca tomorrow.
2.	Emily and Vicky	**b**	they're going to visit the Old Town tomorrow.
3.	We're going	**c**	are travelling around the USA this summer.
4.	I'm not going to stay	**d**	coming to visit us in July.
5.	Tom	**e**	to go swimming tomorrow.
6.	My grandmother's	**f**	going to take a photo of the beach now.
7.	I	**g**	's going to take us to the lake after lunch.
8.	My brother isn't driving	**h**	lunch at half past one.
9.	We're having	**i**	on a campsite this year.
10.	My parents love sightseeing so	**j**	to France in August – he's flying.

3b

Write a few sentences about your next holiday.

....
....
....
....
....
....
....
....
....
....

 **Get it right!**

Look at the sentence below. Then try to correct the mistake.

This present gave to me by my old German friend.

House and home

1 Read the sentences. Choose the correct word for each space, a, b or c.

1. Can you tell me your ...., please?

   a address   **b** apartment   **c** house

2. Many British houses have got .... on the floor.

   a carpet   **b** curtains   **c** downstairs

3. I haven't got a ...., so I have to park my car on the street.

   a gate   **b** garage   **c** roof

4. Some people sing when they are in the ..... .

   a cupboard   **b** sink   **c** shower

5. It was cold last night, so I got an extra .... from the cupboard.

   a blanket   **b** pillow   **c** lamp

6. Oh no! I've lost my house ..... . Can you lend me yours, please?

   a doors   **b** computers   **c** keys

7. My brother lives in a flat on the third .... of a building.

   a door   **b** floor   **c** room

8. I need to go shopping because there isn't any milk in the ..... .

   a book shelves   **b** cooker   **c** fridge

9. There's a comfortable .... in my living room.

   a armchair   **b** bed   **c** television

10. Can you put a clean .... in the bathroom, please?

    a clock   **b** desk   **c** towel

  Exam task

2 ◀)) Track 12

For each question, choose the correct answer.

1 You will hear two friends talking about the man's new apartment. What did he buy for his new apartment?

A bookshelves

B an armchair

C curtains

2 You will hear a boy leaving a message for his mother. Where is the cake?

A on the table

B in the fridge

C on the cooker

3 You will hear a woman talking to her daughter Jodie. Where is Jodie's grandfather now?

   A in the garden

   B in the living room

   C in the garage

4 You will hear a woman talking about her office at home. What will the woman move?

   A a lamp

   B a desk

   C a cupboard

5 You will hear a man and a woman talking at home. What is broken?

   A a clock

   B a radio

   C a television

3 Put the words into the correct order to make questions. Then write answers about where you live.

1. Do / live / you / house / a / or / in / flat / a / ?

....

2. it / How / got / bedrooms / many / has / ?

....

3. What / door / is / your / colour / front / ?

....

4. you / a / Have / garden / got / ?

....

5. TV / you / usually / do / Where / watch / ?

....

6. you / in / got / bedroom / an / Have / armchair / your / ?

....

7. Is / in / there / a / living / your / room / clock / ?

....

8. you / Do / city / in / live / a / ?

....

 Exam facts

- In this part, you listen to one or two people talking.
- There are five questions and you have to choose the right answer (A, B or C).
- You have to answer a question or complete a sentence.

PART 4 🔊 2

Entertainment and the media

1a Write the correct adjective in each gap.

1. The TV programme wasn't interesting –
   we all thought it was b _ _ _ _ g

2. The new comedy play is so f _ _ _ y –
   I laughed all the way through.

3. The action film was so n _ _ _ y – I couldn't
   hear what the actors were saying.

4. There was a story on the news that was really
   s _ _ _ _ _ e – I didn't understand it at all.

5. I love adventure films because they are so
   e _ _ _ _ _ _ g, but my brother thinks they
   are scary.

1b Read the sentences and put the correct job in each gap.

tour guide	journalist	photographer	actor	musician

1. I write articles for newspapers and magazines. I'm a ....

2. I play the guitar in a band. I'm a ....

3. I show visitors around my city. I'm a ....

4. I'm famous because I've acted in many movies. I'm an ....

5. I take pictures for news websites. I'm a ....

 Exam tips

- You will hear information about all three answers, but only one is correct.
- You have to listen for the main idea or the topic or opinions. Make sure you listen to the whole piece before choosing your answer.
- The speaker(s) may use some words that are not from the Key wordlist, but you will not need to understand these to answer the question.

✓ Exam task

2

🔊 Track 13

For each question, choose the correct answer.

1 You will hear two friends talking about going to the theatre. How will the woman travel to the theatre?

  A by car

  B on foot

  C in a taxi

2 You will hear a boy talking about a book he has just read. What did he think about the book?

  A It was funny.

  B It was strange.

  C It was exciting.

3 You will hear two friends agreeing where to meet before a concert. Where will they meet?

  A at the café

  B at the ticket office

  C at the entrance

4 You will hear a woman describing her job. What is her job?

  A tour guide

  B coach driver

  C hotel receptionist

5 You will hear a teacher talking to her class. What does she want the class to do?

  A read something

  B draw something

  C write something

3 Underline the imperatives in the sentences. One of the sentences does not have an imperative. Then match the sentences (1–10) to the people (a–j).

1. Call us now to make an appointment.	**a** a football club
2. Phone Peter on 553442 about the next match.	**b** a hairdresser
3. Look on our webpage for details about the cruise.	**c** a parent
4. Shhh. Don't talk!	**d** a hotel receptionist
5. OK, everyone, show me your homework, please.	**e** a teacher
6. Send me a postcard when you're on holiday!	**f** a travel agent's
7. Please fill in this form before we give you your key.	**g** a tourist information office
8. Thank you. That is the end of the test.	**h** a Cambridge English Speaking examiner
9. Paul, go to bed now!	**i** a student in a library
10. Meet the tour guide outside the museum at 9 a.m.	**j** your friend

Education and study

1 Complete the swimming pool rules with the words in the box.

don't	have (x2)	must (x2)	mustn't	not	to

1. You .... follow these rules.

2. You .... run.

3. You .... have a shower before you get into the pools.

4. You must .... eat or drink in the pools.

5. If you can't swim, you .... to stay in the small pool.

6. If you have short hair, you .... have to wear a swimming hat.

7. Children under five years old don't .... to pay.

8. Children under eight years old have .... be with an adult.

☑ Exam task

2 ◀») Track 14

For each question, choose the correct answer.

1 You will hear a girl telling her uncle about school. What is her favourite subject?

A history

B art

C science

2 You will hear a teacher talking to students. What is different about today's science club?

A the time

B the room

C the teacher

3 You will hear Jim telling his friend why he can't play hockey. What has Jim hurt?

A his hand

B his leg

C his foot

4 You will hear two friends talking at school. What has the girl forgotten to bring to school?

A her bag

B her purse

C her pencil case

5 You will hear a teacher talking to her class about a visit yesterday. Where did they visit?

A an art gallery

B an animal park

C a science museum

Put the words into the correct order to make sentences.

1. You / lots / vegetables / to / of / and / eat / fruit / have / .

....

2. mustn't / in / run / corridors / You / the / !

....

3. for / You / to / take / need / this / ten / medicine / days / .

....

4. have / You / me / don't / to / help / .

....

5. your / turn / You / mobile / an / phone / in / exam / off / must / .

....

6. shout / needn't / I / You / hear / can / you / !

....

Read the sentences and choose the correct alternative for each one.

1. Tom *has / must* to wear a suit to work every day.

2. We *don't have to / mustn't* touch the animals – they're dangerous!

3. Alice *must / need* speak English in the classroom!

4. Dad, you *have to / needn't* take me to the cinema – I can get the bus.

5. Jackie *doesn't have / mustn't* to go to school on Saturday mornings.

6. You *don't have / need* to call your sister this evening – she's worried about you!

 **Get it right!**

Look at the sentences below and choose the correct one.

You must to bring a book and a pencil case.
You have to bring a book and a pencil case.

Food and drink

1 Look at the picture and complete questions (1–4) with the words in the box. Then write questions (5–8).

that these this those

1. What's ....? It's milk.
2. What's ....? It's a cake.
3. What are ....? They're crisps.
4. What are ....? They're biscuits.

5. ....? They're sandwiches.
6. ....? It's cola.
7. ....? They're strawberries.
8. ....? It's water.

☑ Exam task

2 ◀)) Track 15

For each question, choose the correct answer.
You will hear Sarah talking to Mike about a picnic.
What will each person bring to the picnic?

Example

0 Sarah   [G]

People

1 Mike ☐
2 Margaret ☐
3 John ☐
4 Andrea ☐
5 Eric ☐

Food and drink

A apples
B biscuits
C cakes
D cola
E hamburgers
F ice cream
G sandwiches
H strawberries

3a Write *C* (countable) or *UC* (uncountable) next to each word.

1. biscuit _ _	**5.** egg _ _	**9.** milk _ _	**13.** sandwich _ _
2. bread _ _	**6.** grape _ _	**10.** orange _ _	**14.** sausage _ _
3. crisp _ _	**7.** hamburger _ _	**11.** pasta _ _	**15.** sugar _ _
4. cheese _ _	**8.** meat _ _	**12.** salad _ _	**16.** water _ _

3b Choose the correct alternative in each sentence.

1. There isn't much *hamburgers / cheese* in the fridge.

2. There aren't many *oranges / milk* in the supermarket.

3. There are a lot of *biscuits / sugar* in our shopping basket.

4. There is a lot of *sausages / pasta* on my plate!

5. There are a few *apples / sugar* in the cupboard.

6. There is a little *eggs / bread* on the table.

7. There *is / are* a lot of salad in this sandwich!

8. There isn't *many / much* water in the bottle.

9. There are a *few / little* grapes in the bowl.

10. *Are / Is* there any crisps in the bag?

11. There aren't *many / much* sandwiches in the shop.

12. There is a *few / little* meat in the freezer.

☑ **Exam facts**

- In this part, you listen to a conversation between two people who know each other.

- There are five questions, plus an example at the beginning.

- You have to match two lists of information – for example, people to jobs, rooms to furniture, presents to people, books/films to opinions.

Hobbies and shopping

1

Look at the table and read the sentences. Are they TRUE or FALSE?

	Surfing	Playing computer games	Going shopping	Dancing
Agatha	✓✓	✗	✓	✗
Hugh	✓✓✓	✓	✗	✓
Vanessa	✓	✓✓	✗	✓✓✓

1. Agatha likes playing computer games. ....

2. Hugh thinks surfing is more interesting than dancing. ....

3. Vanessa prefers surfing to dancing. ....

4. Agatha enjoys surfing and dancing. ....

5. Hugh's favourite hobby is playing computer games. ....

6. Vanessa is not interested in going shopping. ....

7. Agatha doesn't like playing computer games or dancing. ....

8. Hugh thinks playing computer games is boring. ....

9. Agatha prefers going shopping to dancing. ....

10. Hugh and Vanessa don't enjoy going shopping. ....

☑ *Exam task*

2

🔊 Track 16

For each question, choose the correct answer.
You will hear Sonia talking to Dan about shopping.
What did Sonia buy in each shop?

Example

0 chemist's   D

Shops

1 clothes shop ☐

2 bookshop ☐

3 supermarket ☐

4 sports shop ☐

5 market ☐

Things

A bag

B cake

C flowers

D shampoo

E socks

F towel

G trainers

H trousers

3 Choose the best response to each question, a, b or c.

1. Can I help you?
   a Yes, please.　　　　　　**b** Pleased to meet you.　　　**c** Goodbye.

2. Could I try this on, please?
   a It's £10.　　　　　　　**b** Yes, of course.　　　　　**c** It's very big.

3. Would you like me to put the receipt in the bag?
   a No, thanks.　　　　　　**b** That's nice.　　　　　　**c** It's very heavy.

4. Should I make dinner this evening?
   a No, it's OK. I'll do it.　**b** I don't like it.　　　　　**c** I'll have a ham and cheese pizza,
   　　　　　　　　　　　　　　　　　　　　　　　　　　　　　　　　　 please.

5. Can I take your order?
   a A table for two, please.　**b** OK, thank you.　　　　　**c** Yes. Two hamburgers, please.

6. Would you carry this bag for me, please?
   a Yes, please.　　　　　　**b** Yes, of course.　　　　　**c** No, I wouldn't.

7. Can I have two return tickets to Manchester, please?
   a When do you want to travel?　**b** That's fine.　　　　**c** How much is it?

8. Shall I go to the supermarket this afternoon?
   a Yes, I like chicken.　　　**b** No, we will have chicken　**c** Yes, can you buy some chicken?
   　　　　　　　　　　　　　　　　 for dinner.

9. Could you close the window, please?
   a Yes, are you cold?　　　**b** No, I'm cold.　　　　　　**c** Yes, I'm sorry.

10. Would you like a drink?
    a No, I'm not hungry.　　　**b** No, thanks.　　　　　　　**c** Yes, an ice cream please.

4 Write four sentences about yourself. Use *enjoy / favourite / prefer ... to / don't like.*

1. ....
2. ....
3. ....
4. ....

☑ *Exam tips*

- Before you listen, read the two lists and think about what the conversation might be about.
- In the second list, the words you hear are often different from the words you read.
- You can only use an answer once. When you have used an answer, ~~cross it out~~.

Countries and sports

1 Complete the table with the correct words.

Country	Nationality	Language
(1)	Australian	English
Brazil	**(2)**	Portuguese
The United Kingdom	British	**(3)** ....
(4)	Chinese	Chinese
France	**(5)**	French
(6)	Mexican	Spanish
Italy	Italian	**(7)** ....
Turkey	**(8)**	Turkish

☑ Exam task

2 🔊 Track 17

For each question, choose the correct answer.
You will hear Tanya talking to a friend about a
sports camp.
Which sport did each person try?

Example

0 Tanya   B

People

1 Chris ☐
2 Gina ☐
3 Tom ☐
4 Emma ☐
5 Harry ☐

Sports

A basketball
B climbing
C golf
D horse riding
E sailing
F swimming
G tennis
H windsurfing

3 Put the words in the correct order to make suggestions. Use the responses to help you.

1. don't / Why / we / on / shopping / go / Thursday / ?

....

No, I don't like shopping!

2. go / you / like / to / at / skiing / the / Would / weekend / ?

....

I'd love to, but I have to work.

3. beach / running / morning / on / the / Let's / tomorrow / go /.

....

Good idea!

4. want / to / Do / play / you / tennis / after / school / ?

....

No, sorry. I can't.

5. a / we / movie / Shall / watch / later / ?

....

OK. We can see the new Tom Cruise film.

6. walk / going / What / for / a / park / in / afternoon / about / the / this / ?

....

No, that's boring, but we could go skateboarding instead!

 **Get it right!**

Look at the sentences below. Then try to correct the mistake in each one.

I like listening to musics and watching films.
Did you get much presents?

Personal identification

1 Complete the conversation with the correct phrases.

Ben: Hello. My name's Ben. I've just moved to Newville.

Oliver: (1) ....

Ben: Hi, Oliver. Do you live in Newville?

Oliver: (2) ....

Ben: Oh, really! How often do you play sport there?

Oliver: (3) ....

Ben: What do you do at the weekend?

Oliver: (4) ....

Ben: Is the shopping centre in Newville good?

Oliver: (5) ....

Ben: And what's your favourite place in Newville?

Oliver: (6) ....

a Football and tennis but I'm not very good.

b I'm fine, thanks. And you?

c I usually meet my friends, and we go skateboarding.

d Not very often. I prefer watching football on TV.

e Pleased to meet you. I'm Oliver.

f This park because it's very beautiful.

g I don't really know. I do my shopping online.

h Yes, near the sports centre.

☑ Exam task

2 Put the words in the correct order to make questions or sentences. Ask and answer with a partner.

1 your / What's / name / ?

2 old / How / you / are / ?

3 work / Do / are / student / you / a / or / you / ?

4 you / are / Where / from / ?

5 English / your / Who / teacher / is / ?

6 learning / start / English / When / you / did / ?

7 many / lessons / you / do / How / English / week / have / every / ?

8 much / How / do / get / you / homework / English / ?

9 something / lesson / Please / about / English / an / tell / you / me / enjoyed / .

10 kinds / like / do / What / you / of / watching / programmes / TV / ?

11 TV / do / Where / watch / you / ?

12 you / often / do / How / TV / watch / ?

13 watching / Who / you / like / with / TV / do / ?

14 something / programme / Please / favourite / tell / your / me / TV / about / .

3 Complete the sentences with the correct word. The first letter of each word is given to help you.

1. Bob is your first name and Brown is your s _ _ _ _ _ _ .
2. You are a man. You are married. You have a w _ _ _ .
3. Eric has got a sister but he hasn't got any b _ _ _ _ _ _ _ .
4. Your mum has got a sister. She's your a _ _ _ .
5. My father's father is my g _ _ _ _ _ _ _ _ _ .
6. You've got a child. She's a girl. She's your d _ _ _ _ _ _ _ .
7. I am 15 years old and my brother is 17. We're both t _ _ _ _ _ _ _ _ .
8. Your uncle's got two children. They're your c _ _ _ _ _ _ .
9. The people who live near you are your n _ _ _ _ _ _ _ _ _ .
10. Your mum and dad are your p _ _ _ _ _ _ .

☑ **Exam facts**

- In this part, the examiner asks you questions about yourself.
- The questions are about your name, where you come from, and other things, such as your hobbies, family and studies.
- You only speak to the examiner. You don't speak to the other student.

To watch videos of the complete A2 Key and A2 Key for Schools Speaking tests, go to:
https://keyandpreliminary.cambridgeenglish.org/resources.htm

Daily life

1 Complete the conversation with the words in the box.

afternoon	evening	meeting
morning	o'clock	past	quarter
tomorrow	Tuesday	week

Matt: Hi Maria. I haven't seen you for ages! Are you going to Peter's party this **(1)** .... ? I think it starts at eight **(2)** ....

Maria: No, I have to study tonight because I've got an important maths exam **(3)** ....

Matt: Oh, OK. Good luck!

Maria: Thanks. My exams finish next week, so do you want to play tennis on **(4)** .... ?

Matt: I can't. I'm **(5)** .... Martin to talk about our summer holiday.

Maria: What time are you meeting him?

Matt: At a **(6)** .... to ten. He starts work at midday.

Maria: Why don't we play tennis in the **(7)** .... ? We could meet outside the sports centre at half **(8)** .... four.

Matt: Great! But can you lend me a racket? Mine is broken.

Maria: No problem! See you next **(9)** .... and have fun at the party! Do you want me to phone you in the **(10)** .... , after my exam?

Matt: No! I'll be sleeping!

☑ Exam task

2 Use the words to make complete questions or sentences. Ask and answer with a partner.

Personal information
1 What | name?
2 Do | work | student?
3 How old ?
4 Where | live?

Daily life
5 time | you | get up?
6 Where | usually | lunch?
7 When | go | bed?
8 Who | you | eat dinner ?
9 tell | something about | did yesterday.

Sport
10 Which sports | enjoy playing?
11 Where | you | play sport | your town?
12 Which sports | enjoy watching?
13 Who | you | sport with?
14 tell | something | sport | would like | learn.

3 Put the words in the correct order to make sentences.

1. early / never / get up / I / at / the weekend / .

....

2. reads / brother / My / comics / always / .

....

3. often / on / pizza / We / Saturdays / eat / .

....

4. is / sunny / in / It / the summer / usually / .

....

5. English / always / classes / I / on Mondays / have / .

....

6. I / tired / the evening / in / sometimes / am / .

....

7. at / I / the house / usually / leave / half past eight / .

....

8. rides / dad / a motorbike / My / sometimes / to work / .

....

9. the / never / do / cooking / I / at home / .

....

10. in / I / often / my friends / meet / the evening / .

....

☑ **Exam tips**

- Answer with more than one word. For example, if the examiner asks you 'Where do you live?', don't just say 'Italy'. Say 'I live in Italy' or 'I live in a small village in Italy, not far from Rome'.
- For the last question, the examiner will ask you to speak about one thing. For example, he or she will say, 'Now please tell me something about your favourite hobby'.
- Try to say three things when you answer the *Please tell me about …* question.

To watch videos of the complete A2 Key and A2 Key for Schools Speaking tests, go to:
https://keyandpreliminary.cambridgeenglish.org/resources.htm

Places and buildings

1 Choose the correct word to complete the conversation, a, b or c.

1. Have you bought your ticket to York yet?

No, but my dad is driving me to the .... to get it this afternoon.

a cinema **b** museum **c** bus station

2. What do you do at the weekends?

I love dancing, so I always go to the .... on Fridays.

a supermarket **b** disco **c** theatre

3. Where do you usually meet your friends?

We often spend the whole day in the .... , but we never buy anything!

a library **b** shopping centre **c** park

4. Have you finished writing your postcards yet?

Yes, and now I need to buy some stamps. Where's the .... ?

a department store **b** museum **c** post office

5. What are you doing tomorrow afternoon?

I'm having a surfing lesson at 3 p.m. with my friend at the ....

a beach **b** sports centre **c** swimming pool

6. How often do you go to the .... ?

I do my food shopping there every Friday.

a supermarket **b** café **c** hotel

7. What's your favourite film?

I don't like films. I prefer watching plays at the ....

a theatre **b** school **c** gallery

8. Where do you do sport?

I usually go running in the .... every afternoon.

a swimming pool **b** park **c** shopping centre

9. Do you like reading books?

Yes, I do. I borrow books from the .... every month.

a bookshop **b** library **c** bank

10. Please tell me something about your best friend.

Her name's Rosie and she's a nurse. She works in a ....

a school **b** pharmacy **c** hospital

2

Complete the questions and sentences. Ask and answer with a partner.

1 What's .... name?

2 .... old are you?

3 .... you work or .... you a student?

4 Where .... you live?

5 .... do you go in your town at the weekends?

6 Is .... a swimming pool near your house?

7 How .... parks are there in your town?

8 Where do you .... shopping?

9 Please tell me something .... your favourite place in your town.

10 .... many bedrooms are there in your home?

11 Who .... you live with?

12 Where in your town .... your house?

13 .... do you like most about your home?

14 Please .... me something about your living room.

3

Match the questions (1–8) with the answers (a–h).

1. Do you like going to the theatre? ....
2. How often do you go the cinema? ....
3. When do you usually do sport? ....
4. What do you usually do with your friends? ....
5. Where did you go yesterday afternoon? ....
6. How often do you to the library? ....
7. When do you go shopping? ....
8. How often do you watch sport on TV? ....

a   Every day! I swim one kilometre every morning.

b   Every Saturday! I usually go with my sister and she always buys some new clothes.

c   I sometimes go there to study, but I never borrow books.

d   I went to the art gallery. There were a lot of tourists, but I loved the paintings. Dali's were my favourite.

e   Never! I always go to the stadium to watch my favourite team.

f   Never, because it's very expensive. I like watching films on my computer.

g   We love cooking, so we usually go to the supermarket to get the food and then we make dinner together.

h   Yes, I do. I love watching plays.

◎ Get it right!

Look at the sentence below. Then try to correct the mistake.

What time you can come?

To watch videos of the complete A2 Key and A2 Key for Schools Speaking tests, go to:
https://keyandpreliminary.cambridgeenglish.org/resources.htm

Hobbies and leisure

1 Match the questions (1–8) with the answers (a–h).

1. What time do you leave the house in the morning?	**a** At home, with my family.
2. Do you wear a uniform for work?	**b** Every day, because I work in an office.
3. When do you watch TV?	**c** Some toast and a glass of orange juice.
4. What did you have for breakfast this morning?	**d** Usually around half past eight.
5. Do you listen to the radio?	**e** In the evening, after dinner.
6. Where do you usually have dinner?	**f** No, I don't. I prefer listening to my MP3 player.
7. How often do you send emails?	**g** My friends – we usually go to the gym or the swimming pool.
8. Who do you play sport with?	**h** Yes, I do, because I'm a waitress.

☑ Exam task

2 **Phase 1 Discuss this topic with a partner for 1–2 minutes.**

Here are some pictures that show different free time activities. Do you like these different free time activities? Say why or why not.

Ask and answer these questions about the pictures.

Do you think …

… reading is a good way to spend free time?

… going for a picnic with friends is fun?

… baking is a useful free time activity?

Which of these free time activities do you like best? Why?

Phase 2
Ask and answer these questions with a partner.

When you have free time, do you prefer going out or staying at home? (Why?)

What new activity would you like to start doing during your free time? (Why?)

3

Put the letters in the correct order to make words for months and seasons.

1. Aguuts ....
2. tmuanu ....
3. Dmebeecr ....
4. Fbreruya ....
5. Jyaanru ....

6. yJlu ....
7. bSempetre ....
8. sipgrn ....
9. smuemr ....
10. rweitn ....

 **Exam facts**

Part 2 Phase 1

- In this part, you talk to the other student for 1–2 minutes. You have to look at some pictures and discuss why you like or don't like the different things in the pictures.
- After 1–2 minutes, the examiner will ask you one or more questions about the pictures, including, 'Which … do you like best?'

Part 2 Phase 2

- The examiner will ask you two more questions about the same topic as in Part 2 Phase 1.

Sport

1 Complete the sentences with the correct word from the box.

cycle	go	hit	kick	practise	ride	swim	throw	watch	win

1. When you play basketball, you catch the ball and .... it to the other players.
2. Next year, I'm going to learn to .... a horse.
3. You have to .... the ball with a bat when you play cricket.
4. If you want to be good at sport, you have to .... every day.
5. You must be able to .... if you want to learn to surf.
6. Many people prefer to .... sport on TV at the weekend.
7. I want to .... around the city on my new bike tomorrow.
8. You mustn't .... the ball when you play volleyball.
9. I love playing tennis, but I never .... my matches.
10. In the summer, I usually .... running on the beach.

 **Exam tips**

Part 2 Phase 1

- In this part, talk about all five pictures. Say why you like or don't like each picture.
- Ask the other student what he or she thinks.
- It's not necessary to agree with the other student.

Part 2 Phase 2

- There are no right or wrong answers to the questions. Just give your opinions and remember to say why you think that.

☑ **Exam task**

2 **Phase 1 Discuss this topic with a partner for 1–2 minutes.**

Here are some pictures that show different water sports. Do you like these different water sports? Say why or why not.

Ask and answer these questions about the pictures.

Do you think …

… diving is exciting?

… swimming is healthy?

… sailing is easy?

Which of these water sports do you like best? Why?

Phase 2
Ask and answer these questions with a partner.

Do you prefer watching sport or doing sport? (Why?)

Did you enjoy sport more when you were younger? (Why? / Why not?)

3   **Read a conversation between two students. They are discussing five different sports.**

Use sentences a–e to complete the conversation.

a   Not really. You have to walk too far. What about you?

b   And then you could hurt yourself. But it looks exciting, doesn't it?

c   I agree. In my opinion, tennis is easier to learn than golf.

d   You're right, especially if you want to become really good at both those sports.

e   Yes, really hard. And also I'm a bit scared of horses. What about skiing?

1.   I think learning to ride a horse is very difficult. What do you think?

    ………………………… .

2.   I've never tried skiing, but I think it could be dangerous. You might fall over.

    ………………………… .

3.   Yes, you're right. Would you like to learn to play golf?

    ………………………… .

4.   I think golf's a bit boring. And it's hard to hit the ball very far when you're a beginner.

    ………………………… .

5.   I'm not sure about that. They're both hard to learn.

    ………………………… .

Travel and holidays

1a Put the words in the correct place in the table.

boat	bridge	bus stop	car	catch	drive
driver	helicopter	passenger	roundabout	taxi	
tourist	traffic light	travel	visit	visitor	

A thing	A person	A way to travel	A verb
....	....	....	....
....	....	....	....
....	....	....	....
....	....	....	....

1b Complete the sentences with a word from Exercise 1a. You do not need to use all the words.

1. Lots of visitors to London take a .... trip on the River Thames.
2. I took a .... ride over the Grand Canyon last year – it was fantastic.
3. Often, it is faster to .... by train than by bus.
4. I usually go to work on the bus because there's a .... at the end of my street.
5. You have to stop when a .... is red.
6. In the UK, you can learn to .... when you are 17 years old.

☑ *Exam task*

2 Phase 1 Discuss this topic with a partner for 1–2 minutes.

Here are some pictures that show different holidays. Do you like these different holidays? Say why or why not.

Ask and answer these questions about the pictures.

Do you think …

… holidays in the city are expensive?

… camping holidays are fun?

… visiting old places on holiday is interesting?

Which of these holidays do you like best? Why?

Phase 2
Ask and answer these questions with a partner.

Do you prefer to go on holiday with friends or family? (Why?)

Would you like to go on holiday during the winter? (Why? / Why not?)

3 **Complete the text with the correct words, a, b or c.**

My name's Joshua and I love travelling. I've been to lots places and I've **(1)** .... some amazing people. Actually, last year, I even **(2)** .... a famous actor on the beach in Mexico!
This year I've already **(3)** .... three countries. In January, I saw my sister in Spain, in March, I **(4)** .... to Italy and I've just **(5)** .... home from a holiday with my friends. It was fun but my bag **(6)** .... in the supermarket near our hotel!
This summer I **(7)** .... to California with my cousin. We **(8)** .... a motorbike along Highway One and explore San Francisco. I think we **(9)** .... an amazing time!

1. **a** have met	**b** meet	**c** met
2. **a** seen	**b** saw	**c** see
3. **a** visit	**b** visited	**c** visiting
4. **a** go	**b** gone	**c** went
5. **a** return	**b** returned	**c** returning
6. **a** stole	**b** has stolen	**c** was stolen
7. **a** am going	**b** go	**c** will go
8. **a** are going to ride	**b** ride	**c** 'll ride
9. **a** had	**b** have	**c** 'll have

⊙ Get it right!

Look at the sentences below and and choose the correct one.

Write me a letter to tell me what are you going to do.

Write me a letter to tell me what you are going to do.

 **Think about it** A2 Key Reading and Writing Part 1

Read about A2 Key Reading and Writing Part 1. Are the sentences TRUE or FALSE?

1. In this part of the exam, I have to match short texts with the correct meaning. ....

2. I need to understand the main message of each short text ....

3. There are eight short texts in total. ....

4. For each short text, there are two sentences. ....

5. The short texts can be notices, signs, labels, text messages, emails or notes. ....

6. All of the words in the question will be from the Key wordlist. ....

7. For each question, I only need to mark the correct letter on my answer sheet. ....

8. There is an example at the beginning of A2 Key Reading and Writing Part 1. ....

 **Think about it** A2 Key Reading and Writing Part 2

Complete the sentences about A2 Key Reading and Writing Part 2 with the correct alternatives.

In A2 Key Reading and Writing Part 2, you will be asked to read three short texts. The number of words in each text is **(1)** *always / not always* the same. There might be **(2)** *lots of / a few* words in the texts which are not in the Key wordlist, **(3)** *but you won't / and you will* need to understand these to answer the questions correctly. There are **(4)** *six / seven* questions to answer, with three possible answers for each question (A, B or C). The three texts will **(5)** *always / sometimes* be about three people. The words in the questions may be found in all three texts, so you need to read the texts very **(6)** *quickly / carefully* before you choose your answer. But sometimes the answers in the texts use different words to the questions, so you need to think about other ways of saying the same thing. For example, 'it cost a lot of money' is another way of saying **(7)** *it was cheap / it was expensive*.

Think about it   A2 Key Reading and Writing Part 3

Complete each sentence about A2 Key Reading and Writing Part 3 Sections 1 and 2 with a number from the box.

| one (x4)   two   three   four   five (x2)   250 |

1. In A2 Key Reading and Writing Part 3, there is .... long text to read.

2. The text usually has .... or .... paragraphs.

3. The text could be a newspaper, magazine or online article and it is usually about .... words long.

4. Opposite the text there are .... questions.

5. Each question has .... possible answers for you to choose from.

6. For each question, only .... of the possible answers is correct.

7. This part tests understanding of main ideas and detailed information. Sometimes a question may test feelings, or there may be .... or .... questions which test the writer's opinion.

8. Sometimes you will have to answer .... question about the whole text (for example, *What is the writer doing in this text? / What is the best title for this text?*).

Think about it   A2 Key Reading and Writing Part 4

Complete the information about A2 Key Reading and Writing Part 4 with the words in the box.

| six   gap   encyclopedia   all   vocabulary   three   sentence   topic |

1. A2 Key Reading and Writing Part 4 is mostly a test of .... , but some grammar may also be tested.

2. The text might be information from a news story or from an ....

3. You have to choose the correct word for each .... in the text.

4. For each question, you choose from .... possible answers.

5. There are .... questions to answer altogether.

6. It's a good idea to just read the text first. This gives you an idea of the .... and the general meaning of the whole text.

7. As you answer each question, read the whole .... to help you choose the correct answer.

8. .... of the words in Part 4 are in the A2 Key wordlist.

 **Think about it** A2 Key Reading and Writing Part 5

Complete the sentences about A2 Key Reading and Writing Part 5 with the verbs in the box.

answer	choose	fill	read	show	spell	think	write

In A2 Key Reading and Writing Part 5, you have to **(1)** .... a short text or two short texts, and **(2)** ....
in the gaps. The texts will usually be emails, letters or notes. If there are two texts, the second will be a response
to the first. For example, the first text might be an invitation, and the second text will **(3)** .... that invitation.
There are ten gaps to fill in, plus an example to **(4)** .... you what to do. There are no words to **(5)** ....
from – you have to **(6)** .... of the missing word. You should **(7)** .... only one word in each gap, and
you must **(8)** .... the word correctly. Part 5 tests grammar, and the missing words will usually be auxiliary
verbs, modal verbs, prepositions, pronouns or determiners.

 **Think about it** A2 Key Reading and Writing Part 6

Match the questions (1–5) about A2 Key Reading and Writing Part 6 with the answers (a–e).

1. Is A2 Key Reading and Writing Part 6 a reading or writing exercise?

2. What type of message do I need to write?

3. What information do I need to include?

4. How long should my answer be?

5. Can I write more words than the question asks for?

a You need to write an email to a friend.

b You must write 25 words or more.

c It is a writing task.

d Yes, but you only need to answer the three questions/instructions to get full marks. Don't spend too long on Part 6 because you need time for Part 7.

e You will see three short questions or instructions. You need to answer all of them in your email.

Read about A2 Key Reading and Writing Part 7. Are the sentences TRUE or FALSE?

1. In this part of the exam, I have to write an article. ....

2. I need to write 35 words or more. ....

3. There are four pictures to look at. ....

4. I must write about the main events of the pictures. ....

5. To get full marks, my spelling, grammar and vocabulary must be perfect. ....

6. If I write 100 words, I will get full marks. ....

7. It's a good idea to use more than one paragraph and/or linking words. ....

8. I should write my story on a piece of paper before writing the final answer on my answer sheet. ....

 **Think about it** A2 Key Listening Part 1

Match 1–8 with a–h to make sentences about A2 Key Listening Part 1.

1.	In A2 Key Listening Part 1, there are	**a**	or a shop assistant and a customer, for example.
2.	Every question has	**b**	between two people.
3.	You have to	**c**	choose one answer for each question, A, B or C.
4.	You will hear a conversation	**d**	five questions.
5.	The conversations may be between friends or relatives,	**e**	three answer options, based on pictures.
6.	You need to listen for important information, such as	**f**	each conversation twice.
7.	You will hear	**g**	times, prices, days of the week or numbers.
8.	You need to choose and write your answers	**h**	while you are listening to the conversations.

 **A2 Key Listening Part 2**

Read the sentences about A2 Key Listening Part 2. Are the answers TRUE or FALSE?

1. In A2 Key Listening Part 2, you will hear two people talking. ....

2. The speakers will always have a British accent. ....

3. You will complete a message or notes with information. ....

4. You need to choose from A, B or C answers. ....

5. The answer will always be one word. ....

6. You can make spelling mistakes in this part of the exam. ....

7. There are five gaps to complete in a text. ....

8. The speakers might spell some of the difficult words. ....

 **A2 Key Listening Part 3**

Read the sentences about A2 Key Listening Part 3 and choose the correct alternatives.

1. In A2 Key Listening Part 3, you answer the questions by *choosing A, B or C / writing a word*.

2. You listen to *one long conversation / five short conversations*.

3. You listen to *two / four* people talking.

4. There are *five / eight* questions to answer.

5. The speakers *know / don't know* each other.

6. The speakers talk about *school, university or work / something they are interested in*.

7. You must choose *one answer / two answers* for each question.

8. You are given *one point / two points* for every correct answer.

 A2 Key Listening Part 4

Read the paragraph about A2 Key Listening Part 4 and answer the questions.

In Part 4 of the A2 Key Listening test, you have to answer five questions. You will hear five short conversations (with 2 speakers) or monologues (just 1 speaker). The question describes what the situation is, for example it could be two friends or family members, or the speakers could be strangers, for example a shop assistant and a customer. You are listening for the main idea or the topic, and you need to choose from A, B or C answers. Most of the words and grammatical structures will be from the A2 Key wordlist or the list of Grammatical Areas in the A2 Key Handbook. A speaker may use a few words and/or grammatical structures that are higher than A2 Key level. However, it should be possible to get the correct answer even if you don't understand every word. You should write on the question paper while you are listening.

1. How many questions are there in A2 Key Listening Part 4?

2. How many speakers will there be in each question?

3. Who might the speakers be?

4. What sort of information are you listening for?

5. Is all the vocabulary you will hear from the A2 Key wordlist?

6. Where do you have to write your answers while you are listening?

 A2 Key Listening Part 5

Complete the information about A2 Key Listening Part 5 with the words in the box.

activities	answer	daily	eight	end	five	question	simple	twice	two

In A2 Key Listening Part 5, you need to understand a **(1)** .... conversation between **(2)** .... people. They might be talking about topics such as free time **(3)** .... , travel or **(4)** .... life. You will hear the conversation **(5)** .... There are **(6)** .... questions and you have to choose from **(7)** .... options. You should write your answers on the **(8)** .... paper while you listen and you have time at the **(9)** .... of the Listening test to write your answers onto the **(10)** .... sheet in pencil.

 **Think about it** A2 Key Speaking Part 1

Read the paragraph about A2 Key Speaking Part 1 and answer the questions with the words in the box. You do not need to use all the words.

In the A2 Key Speaking test, there will be two examiners in the room, but only one of the examiners will talk to you. The other examiner will only listen to you. In Part 1, you need to listen to the examiner and answer their questions. There will be another student (or maybe two students) in the room, but in this part of the Speaking test, you only need to talk to the examiner.

Part 1 has two Phases: Phase 1 and Phase 2. In Phase 1, you will have to give your name, but you do not need to spell it. Next, the examiner asks you your age (in A2 Key for Schools) or if you work or study (in A2 Key). After that, you are asked where you are from or where you live. In Phase 2, the examiner will ask you some questions about two topics. These questions are about your daily life (for example, food, free time, the weather, friends/family, home). For each topic, both students have two short questions to answer. In other words, the examiner asks four short questions per topic. Then, at the end of each topic, one student answers a longer question that begins *Now, please tell me something about … .*

the other student	shorter	name	listens	two	four
the examiner	hobbies	age	nationality	longer	talks

1. There are two examiners in the Speaking test: one who asks the questions and one who only ....

2. In Speaking Part 1, you speak to ....

3. In Part 1 Phase 1, first you are asked your ....

4. In Part 1 Phase 1, you will be asked either about your .... or about your job / studies. Then you are asked where you are from / where you live.

5. In Part 1 Phase 2, the examiner asks you personal questions about .... different topics.

6. At the end of each topic, the examiner asks a .... question.

 **Think about it** A2 Key Speaking Part 2

Read the text. Then match the questions (1–6) about the A2 Key Speaking test Part 2 with the answers (a–f).

A2 Key Speaking Part 2 has two phases: Phase 1 and Phase 2.

In Phase 1, you and the other student have a discussion for 1 to 2 minutes. The examiner gives you five pictures to talk about and tells you the topic (e.g. sport, holidays, TV programmes). You have to say why you like or don't like the things in the pictures. If you can't talk for 2 minutes, the examiner will ask you one or more questions about the pictures. At the end of Part 2 Phase 1, the examiner will ask which of the things in the pictures you like best.

In Part 2 Phase 2, the examiner will ask two more discussion questions on the same topic as in Phase 1. You and the other student are asked the same questions.

Part 2 Phase 1

1. Who do you have to talk to in Part 2 Phase 1?

2. How long do you have to speak for?

3. What will happen if you don't speak for all the time you have?

4. After you finish speaking about the pictures, what will the examiner ask you?

Part 2 Phase 2

5. How many questions are there in Part 2 Phase 2?

6. What will the questions be about?

a The examiner will ask you a question about one of the pictures.

b The same topic as Part 2 Phase 1.

c The other student.

d Only two.

e Between one and two minutes.

f Which (picture) you like best.

Appliances

camera	DVD (player)	laptop	telephone
CD (player)	electric	lights	television / TV
cell phone	electricity	mobile (phone)	video
clock	fridge	MP3 player	washing machine
computer	gas	PC	
cooker	heating	phone	
digital camera	lamp	radio	

Clothes and Accessories

bag	fashion	purse	swimsuit
bathing suit	get dressed	raincoat	tie
belt	glasses	ring	tights
blouse	glove	scarf	trainers
boot	handbag	sock	trousers
bracelet	hat	shirt	try on (v)
cap	jacket	shoes	T-shirt
chain	jeans	shorts	umbrella
clothes	jewellery / jewelry	skirt	uniform
coat	jumper	suit	wallet
costume (swimming)	kit	sunglasses	watch
dress	necklace	sweater	wear (v)
earring	pocket	swimming costume	

Colours

black	golden	pale	white
blue	green	pink	yellow
bright	grey	purple	
brown	light	red	
dark	orange	silver	

Communication and Technology

address	chatroom	download (n & v)	keyboard
at / @	click (v)	DVD (player)	laptop (computer)
by post	computer memory	email (n & v)	mobile (phone)
call (v)	computer	envelope	mouse
camera	conversation	file	MP3 player
CD (player)	digital	information	net
cell phone	digital camera	internet	online
chat	dot	internet site	password

PC	post something online	talk	video
phone	printer	telephone	web
photograph	screen	text (n & v)	web page
photography	software	upload	website

Documents and Texts

ad / advertisement	diploma	message	project
article	email	newspaper	sign
bill	form	note	text (n & v)
book	letter	notebook	textbook
card	licence	notice	ticket
comic	magazine	passport	
diary	menu	postcard	

Education

advanced	course	lesson	ruler
beginner	desk	level	school
biology	dictionary	library	science
blackboard	diploma	mark	student
board	eraser	maths / mathematics	studies
book	exam(ination)	note	study (v)
bookshelf	geography	physics	subject
chemistry	history	practice (n)	teach
class	homework	practise (v)	teacher
classmate	information	project	term
classroom	instructions	pupil	test (n)
clever	know	read	university
coach	language	remember	
college	learn	rubber	

Entertainment and Media

act	CD (player)	drawing	hip hop
actor	chess	drum	instrument
adventure	cinema	DVD (player)	keyboard
advertisement	classical (music)	exhibition	laugh
art	competition	festival	listen to
article	concert	film (n & v)	look at
board game	dance (n & v)	fun	magazine
book	dancer	go out	MP3 player
card	disco	group	museum
cartoon	draw	guitar	music

musician	photography	project	singer
news	piano	radio	song
newspaper	picture	rap music	television / TV
opera	play (n)	read (v)	theatre
paint (v)	pop (music)	rock (concert)	ticket
painter	practice (n)	screen (n)	video (game)
photograph	practise (v)	show (n)	watch (v)
photographer	programme	sing	

Family and Friends

aunt	girl	group	Ms
boy	grandchild	guest	mum(my)
brother	grand(d)ad	guy	neighbour
child	granddaughter	husband	parent
cousin	grandfather	love (n & v)	penfriend
dad(dy)	grandma	married	sister
daughter	grandmother	Miss	son
family	grandpa	mom	surname
father	grandparent	mother	teenager
friend	grandson	Mr	uncle
friendly	granny	Mrs	wife

Food and Drink

apple	cafe / café	cooker	food
bake	cafeteria	cookie	fork
banana	cake	cooking	French fries
barbecue	can (n)	cream	fresh
bean	candy	cup	fridge
biscuit	carrot	curry	fried
boil	cereal	cut (n)	fruit
boiled	cheese	delicious	garlic
bottle	chef	dessert	glass
bowl	chicken	dinner	grape
box	chilli	dish (n)	grilled
bread	chips	drink	honey
break (n)	chocolate	eat	hungry
breakfast	coffee	egg	ice
burger	cola	fast food	ice cream
butter	cook (n & v)	fish	jam

juice	mineral water	potato	strawberry
kitchen	mushroom	restaurant	sugar
knife	oil	rice	supper
lemon	omelette	roast (v & adj)	sweet (n & adj)
lemonade	onion	salad	tea
lunch	orange	salt	thirsty
lunchtime	order a meal	sandwich	toast
main course	pasta	sauce	tomato
mango	pear	sausage	vegetable
meal	pepper	serve	waiter
meat	picnic	slice (n)	waitress
melon	piece of cake	snack (n)	wash up
menu	pizza	soup	water
milk	plate	steak	yog(h)urt

Health, Medicine and Exercise

accident	danger	hair	problem
ambulance	dangerous	hand	rest (n)
appointment	dead	head	run
arm	dentist	health	sick
baby	die	hear (v)	soap
back	doctor	heart	stomach
blood	Dr	hospital	stomach ache
body	ear	hurt (v)	swim
brain	exercise	ill	temperature
break (v)	eye	leg	tired
check (v)	face	lie down	tooth
chemist	fall (v)	medicine	toothache
clean (adj & v)	feel (v)	neck	toothbrush
cold (n)	finger	nose	walk
comb (n)	fit	nurse	well (adj)
cut (v)	foot	pain	

Hobbies and Leisure

barbecue	camera	club	draw
beach	camp	collect (v)	DVD (player)
bicycle	camping	computer	festival
bike	campsite	cycling	go out
book	CD (player)	dance (n & v)	go shopping

guitar	member	paint **(n & v)**	quiz
hobby	MP3 player	park	tent
holidays	museum	party	video game
join	music	photograph **(n & v)**	
magazine	musician	picnic	

House and Home

address	closet	garage	refrigerator
apartment	computer	garden	roof
armchair	cooker	gas	room
bath(tub)	cupboard	gate	rubbish
bathroom	curtain	hall	safe **(adj)**
bed	desk	heating	sheet
bedroom	dining room	home	shelf
bin	door	house	shower
blanket	downstairs	key	sink
bookcase	drawer	kitchen	sitting room
bookshelf	DVD (player)	lamp	sofa
bowl	entrance	light	stay **(v)**
box	flat **(n)**	live **(v)**	toilet
carpet	floor	living room	towel
chair	fridge	oven	wall
clock	furniture	pillow	

Measurements

centimetre /	half	litre / liter	second
centimeter / cm	hour	metre / meter	temperature
day	kilo(gram[me]) / kg	minute	week
degree	kilometre / km /	moment	year
gram(me)	kilometer	quarter	

Personal Feelings, Opinions and Experiences (adjectives)

able	better	careful	famous
afraid	big	clear	fast
alone	bored	clever	favourite
amazing	boring	cool	fine
angry	brave	different	free
bad	brilliant	difficult	friendly
beautiful	busy	excellent	funny

good	lucky	real	tall
great	married	rich	terrible
happy	modern	right	tired
hard	nice	slow	unhappy
heavy	noisy	small	useful
high	old	soft	well
hungry	pleasant	sorry	worried
important	poor	special	wrong
interested	pretty	strange	young
interesting	quick	strong	
kind	quiet	sure	
lovely	ready	sweet	

Places: Buildings

apartment (building)	department store	hospital	railway station
bank	disco	hotel	school
block	elevator	house	shop
bookshop	entrance	library	sports centre
bookstore	exit	lift	stadium
building	factory	museum	supermarket
cafe / café	flat	office	swimming pool
cafeteria	garage	pharmacy	theatre
castle	grocery store	police station	university
cinema	guesthouse	port	
college	harbour	post office	

Places: Countryside

area	forest	path	sky
beach	hill	railway	village
campsite	island	rainforest	wood
farm	lake	river	
field	mountain	sea	

Places: Town and City

airport	city centre	petrol station	station
bridge	corner	playground	street
bus station	market	road	town
bus stop	motorway	roundabout	underground
car park	park	square	zoo

Services

bank	doctor	petrol station	theatre
cafe / café	garage	post office	tourist information centre
cafeteria	hotel	restaurant	
cinema	library	sports centre	
dentist	museum	swimming pool	

Shopping

ad / advertisement	close **(v)**	go shopping	shop assistant
assistant	closed	open **(v & adj)**	shopper
bill	cost **(n & v)**	pay (for)	shopping
bookshop	credit card	penny	spend
buy **(v)**	customer	pound	store
cash **(n & v)**	department store	price	supermarket
cent	dollar	receipt	try on
change **(n & v)**	euro	rent	
cheap	expensive	sale	
cheque	for sale	shop	

Sport

ball	fishing	ride **(n & v)**	swimming
badminton	football	riding	swimming costume
baseball	football player	rugby	swimming pool
basketball	game	run **(v)**	swimsuit
bat	goal	sailing	table tennis
bathing suit	golf	sea	team
beach	gym	skate **(v)**	tennis
bicycle	hockey	skateboard **(n)**	tennis player
bike	keep fit	ski **(v)**	throw **(v)**
boat	kit	skiing	ticket
catch **(v)**	luck	snowboard **(n)**	tired
climb **(v)**	member	snowboarding	trainers
club	play **(v)**	soccer	v / versus
coach **(n)**	player pool	sport(s)	volleyball
competition	practice **(n)**	sports centre	walk **(v)**
cricket	practise **(v)**	stadium	watch **(v)**
cycling	prize	surf	win **(v)**
enter (a competition)	race **(n & v)**	surfboard	windsurfing
equipment	racket	surfboarding	winner
exercise **(n & v)**	rest **(n & v)**	swim	

The Natural World

air	dolphin	insect	space
animal	duck	island	spring
autumn	east	lake	star
beach	elephant	moon	summer
bear	explorer	mountain	tiger
bee	field	mouse	tree
bird	fire	nature	water
butterfly	fish	north	west
camel	flower	plant	whale
chicken	forest	rabbit	wild animal
country	grass	river	winter
countryside	grow	sea	wood
cow	hill	sheep	wool
desert	horse	sky	world
dinosaur	hot	snake	
dog	ice	south	

Time

afternoon	evening	morning	tonight
a.m. / p.m.	half (past)	night	week
appointment	holidays	noon	weekday
autumn	hour	o'clock	weekend
birthday	January – December	past	weekly
calendar	meeting	quarter (past / to)	winter
century	midnight	second	working hours
clock	minute	spring	year
daily	moment	summer	yesterday
date	Monday – Sunday	time	
day	month	today	
diary	monthly	tomorrow	

Travel and Transport

(aero) / (air)plane	bus stop	driver	fly
airport	car	driving / driver's	garage
ambulance	case	licence	helicopter
backpack	coach	engine	journey
boat	country	engineer	leave
bridge	delay (n & v)	explorer	left
bus	delayed	far	light
bus station	drive	flight	luggage

machine

map

mechanic

mirror

miss **(v)**

motorbike

motorway

move

oil

park **(v)**

passenger

passport

petrol

petrol station

pilot

platform

railway

repair **(v)**

return **(n & v)**

ride

right

road

roundabout

sailing

seat

ship

station

stop

straight on

street

suitcase

taxi

ticket

tour **(n)**

tour guide

tourist

tourist information

 centre

traffic

traffic light

train

tram

travel

trip

tyre

underground **(n)**

visit

visitor

way **(n)**

wheel

window

Weather

cloud

cloudy

cold

fog

foggy

hot

ice

rain

snow

storm

sun

sunny

thunderstorm

warm

weather

wet

wind

windy

Work and Jobs

actor

artist

boss

break **(n)**

business

business person

businessman

businesswoman

chemist

cleaner

coach **(n)**

company

computer

cook **(n & v)**

customer

dentist

desk

diary

diploma

doctor

Dr

driver

earn

email **(n & v)**

engineer

explorer

factory

farm

farmer

footballer

football player

guest

guide

instructions

job

journalist

king

letter

manager

mechanic

meeting

message

musician

nurse

occupation

office

painter

photographer

pilot

police officer

queen

receptionist

secretary

shop assistant

shopper

singer

staff

student

teacher

tennis player

tour guide

uniform

waiter / waitress

work

worker

writer

ACKNOWLEDGEMENTS

The authors and publishers acknowledge the following sources of copyright material and are grateful for the permissions granted. While every effort has been made, it has not always been possible to identify the sources of all the material used, or to trace all copyright holders. If any omissions are brought to our notice, we will be happy to include the appropriate acknowledgements on reprinting and in the next update to the digital edition, as applicable.

Keys: RW = Reading and Writing, L = Listening, S = Speaking, P = Part

Photography

All the images are sourced from Getty Images.

RWP1: Wavebreakmedia Ltd; Glowimages; **RWP2**: Martyn Ferry/Moment; FatCamera/E+; Peter Durant/ Passage; **RWP3**: martin-dm/E+; 1111IESPDJ/E+; jeffbergen/E+; Ogphoto/E+; **RWP4**: Jupiterimages/ Stockbyte; simonkr/E+; 8213erika/iStock/Getty Images Plus; Kenny Bengtsson/Folio; **RWP5**: Andersen Ross/DigitalVision; ake1150sb/iStock/Getty Images Plus; Sarah Fix/DigitalVision; Erik Isakson; Geri Lavrov/Moment Open; william87/iStock/Getty Images Plus; **RWP6**: BraunS/E+; Steve Debenport/E+; John Eder/Stone; **RWP7**: RubberBall Productions/Brand X Pictures; **L2**: Marco Simoni/robertharding; PhotoAlto/Frederic Cirou/PhotoAlto Agency RF Collections; emilywineman/E+; **L3**: Howard Kingsnorth/ Cultura Exclusive; monkeybusinessimages/iStock/Getty Images Plus; izusek/E+; m-imagephotography/ iStock/Getty Images Plus; **L4**: Jose Luis Pelaez Inc/DigitalVision; **L5**: franckreporter/E+; Don Mason/ Blend Images; Colin Hawkins/Cultura; **S1**: Image Source; MoMo Productions/DigitalVision; Eva Katalin Kondoros/E+; Diane Auckland/Passage.

Illustrations

QBS Learning

Audio

Audio production by Hart McLeod, Cambridge and by DN and AE Strauss Ltd. Cambridge.